THE ART OF DYING WELL

Neil Cabe, Ph.D.

ISBN NUMBER 978-1502782243

Printed in the United States of America

Kindle Edition © 2007, 2011

Paperback Edition © 2014

Table of Contents

Acknowledgements

For my wife Jean, who has tolerated my musings for years. More importantly, she has spent untold hours sitting quietly by the side of my various hospital beds, comforting, seeing me through my fears and pains, and often feeding me Jell-O. I cannot thank her enough. My life would be less than half a life without her.

My friend and first reader Abigail Nussey, even while working on her own dissertation, took the time to encourage me, correct me, and guide me in my own process. I am extremely grateful to her.

Finally, the large number of persons who have read the earlier edition of this little book have been extremely encouraging and supportive of its re-printing. Many have told me it was helpful to them in their own process, and in dealing with the dying of those they have loved. They, truly, are the inspiration for this.

Part I: My Story

Somebody should tell us, right at the start
of our lives that we are dying. Then we might live life to the limit,
every minute of every day. Do it! I say.
Whatever you want to do, do it now!
There are only so many tomorrows.
-- Pope Paul VI

I am dying.

This is not a case of "We all begin dying the day we are born." or "All of us will die someday." Three years ago, a cardiac surgeon said that I had at best five years to live, and that I stood a very good chance of dying within two. This is my story.

I do not really look like I am dying – whatever that means. At least this is what others often tell me, perhaps out of concern for my feelings. I hope this little book makes it clear that I am at peace with that prognosis. I have done, and am doing, the things I suggest in these pages.

You see, we all have what is called an ejection fraction – that is the amount of blood pumped out by our hearts on any given beat. In a healthy heart, the ejection fraction is generally between 55% and 65%. Mine is 15%, and has remained so for more than the last two years. The five-year mortality rate, really the death rate, for those of us with an ejection fraction of 35% or less is about 50%. The two-year mortality rate for an ejection fraction of 15% is around 85%. The second group is my own, but I've made it past two years.

In the time since my diagnosis, I have done everything I can to lengthen my life. I have followed my doctors' orders completely, I take all of my medications (14 pills each day, at last count) on schedule, and I have changed my lifestyle to be as heart-healthy as I can. I have lost over 50 pounds, my cholesterol has dropped to about 100, and all of my current blood work is nearly perfect. I drink no alcohol, and very seldom eat red meat. I am now almost a vegetarian, but contentedly so.

It all began simply enough. My family doctor ordered a stress test based solely on my age and physical condition. I flunked. Following that, he sent me to some excellent cardiac care professionals, who recommended stents. On further examination, my cardiac surgeon decided, and told me, that stents would do no good. Further tests showed the need for a triple by-pass, which became a quadruple by-pass during surgery, and uncovered two older heart attacks and atrophied heart muscle as a result. I have often wondered what it is like to hold another person's heart in your hands, as that man did mine.

Then a revealing experience that nearly killed me changed not only my outlook on myself, but also on the world at large. It gave me a better sense of my place in my own history, and a wonderful sense of my place in the lives of those I love.

About three days following the heart surgery, I came to my wife who was standing in the kitchen, and announced to her as gently but urgently as I could, that I was suffocating. She is a trooper in a crisis. She called the hospital and told them to meet us at the door with a wheel chair and oxygen, which they did. An x-ray immediately showed my heart as extremely enlarged, which was later diagnosed as pericarditis – in infection of the sac around the heart – which is deadly.

The ER doctor (Who, by the way, played football for me when he was 14 and I was his coach, 30 years ago.) called for the Med-Evac helicopter. Nurses rolled me out in the rain to the waiting helicopter, and I was flown to the hospital where my bypass had been performed. During the 12-minute ride, I eased up on one elbow and looked down through rain-spattered windows at the city where I had grown up. It was beautiful. Lying back down, I thought, 'What if this is the end? What if I die tonight?' In just a moment, I relaxed in peace, and I now know why. It was contentment, which I will explain later.

The surgeon who had done the by-pass was called in at midnight, and performed what is called a cardiac window, really just poking a hole in the pericardium, and allowing it to drain. A normal amount of fluid around the heart is about 50 cc's. He removed 600 cc's from around my heart, and told me later that I was perhaps thirty minutes from death. The next day, they removed one and one-half liters of fluid from around my lungs, where there is supposed to be essentially none.

The next year, a pacemaker was installed, followed by its removal and replacement with a pacemaker/defibrillator. About a year later, the defibrillator fired one night while I was in the bathroom. I was sure at the time that I had urinated on an open electrical wire, which of course was impossible! My wife and I called the emergency room, and I was told to come to the community hospital for an electrocardiogram. While I was brushing my teeth before that visit, it fired again.

If you have a defibrillator, and it has ever fired, you alone know the sensation. It is as if you have been hit with a Taser, from the inside of your chest. Very strange. I stayed in the hospital for four days following those episodes, and it was then that I received my diagnosis.

I can't speak for all cardio-vascular surgeons, but mine had a bedside manner about like Count Dracula on a bad day. He stood way over in the corner of the room, about as far away from me as he could get, and announced to me that the news was bad, and that I had about five years to live. Unceremoniously, and without even a "gosh-that's-too-bad", he left the room, and I was alone, with my wife hovering in the corner.

So, I am dying. The only cure for my condition is a heart transplant. In time, I will grow weak enough that I will have great trouble walking from one room to the next, and climbing stairs will be out of the question. Even now, more than one flight of stairs is a cause for a pounding heart and need for rest. Performing even the simplest

4

of tasks will become extremely difficult, and lifting over only a few pounds will become a challenge not to be taken lightly. I have to carry only one or two bags of groceries at a time from the car to the kitchen. For now, one day at a time, and in small ways I cannot know, cannot see, and am only now beginning to feel, I am slowly dying.

I did not know how to deal with the business of dying. How should I feel? How should I react? What do I tell my friends and family? What, really, does dying mean? How do you _do_ this? And, perhaps most importantly, what has my life meant? I have struggled with these questions, and others. At the beginning, I could find no answers.

Those who work with the dying, who work in hospice care, and some of those who survive the death of a loved one, have written a number of books. I have found nothing that speaks directly from the heart of one who *is* dying, to the hearts of *others* who are in the same condition, regardless of the cause of impending death. It is a rare and extraordinary air that we breathe. Eventually though, we all must inhale.

In the pages that follow, I want to try to share my journey with you. Perhaps it will help you to deal with your own dying; perhaps it will help those who are a part of the dying process with others.

William James is quoted as having said, "The best use of life is to spend it for something that outlasts it" (James, 2011). What have I learned in my life – and in my illness – that might benefit others? And, how can I share the things I now know to be true? I do not in any way believe that I am a special human being, though I hope some few people in my life see me that way. I am only a man, as you are only man or woman. We are none of us unique. But perhaps those of us who are dying have a perspective that is unique.

One of the truly irritating things about my own illness has been the reaction of others. They are all so future-focused that they tend too often to ignore both the reality of the present moment, and the treasures of the past.

To be sure, we have all misused moments in our histories, and are often rightly ashamed or guilty for some things we have done. But are we equally joyful over loves we have loved, good deeds we have done, prayers we have prayed, silent and tender moments we have shared with others who needed us? And have we not suffered in the past, and done so with dignity and honor? I believe the majority of us spend so much time looking forward, that we have forgotten the wonderful moments of our own history, while at the same time missing the importance of the present. No one can ever erase the treasures of our past. And as long as I continue to live, I may choose to right the wrongs I have committed, and more importantly I hope I choose my attitude toward this suffering moment, so that it becomes a monument both to who I was, and to who I am while I still live.

I believe there is randomness to the universe, and in each of our own private realities. I do not believe that all things necessarily happen for a reason. Bette Davis is sometimes quoted as having said, 'Old age ain't for sissies!' There may be no greater good to be served by my illness or yours, no point to the vagaries of old age, no justice in the heartaches of Alzheimer's or breast cancer. These are not the "will of God", any more than they are "works of the devil". They are simply facts of life, and facts with which we must deal. God will not

6

interfere with the will of man or the laws of nature. Some things just happen. The physical and natural laws of the universe are undeniable and unmoving. We all make choices in how to approach such a powerful force, and in it we may triumph, no matter how threatening those forces may seem.

Part II: The Meaning and Use of Our Suffering

You know quite well, deep within you,

that there is only a single magic, a single power, a single salvation

...and that is called loving. Well, then, love your suffering.

Do not resist it; do not flee from it.

It is your aversion that hurts, nothing else.

-- Hermann Hesse

As we suffer, we may become imprisoned by it, with too often no vivid memory of our past, and no clear vision of our future. Our apprehension is that there is no future for us, while there _is_ still time future – without us in it. For us, there is only now. And our history, both our personal and community history, is what remains.

The ideas others use by which to live do not apply to those of us who know we are dying. We do not look unrealistically at the future; we are the ultimate realists. For example, while there may be advances in heart surgery and transplantation, they most likely will not come before I die. While AIDS may one day be cured, it will not be before millions more die. Our connections with both the past and the future will soon be irrevocably broken.

Nevertheless, I believe we are responsible for a future lacking only our presence – not our impact on it. The impact of impending death plunges many of us into complacency and stagnation. For some that impact becomes paralyzing, a life without direction. Urgency implies an impulse to action. Too often, we who are dying have lost such urgency. We must find a way "to transcend the limitations of being human" (Nouwen, p. 13). We are seeking a new immortality. But what is it?

Let me tell you about a place I have visited. The American Indians have many stories about a cave in the Black Hills that blows a constant wind. Tipi rings near the natural entrance indicate that the Native Americans knew of Wind Cave. In 1881, two settlers, Jesse and Tom Bingham, were also attracted to the whistling sound of the wind coming from the cave entrance. As the story goes, the wind was blowing out of the cave with such force that it blew off Tom's hat. A few days later when Jesse returned to show this phenomenon to some friends, he was surprised to find the wind had switched directions and his hat was sucked into the cave. Today, we understand that the direction of the wind is related to the difference in atmospheric pressure between the cave and the surface. Scientifically, higher energy states move toward lower energy states. Nature is always trying to balance. But for the American Indian, the cave breathes, and it pulses with the breath of God. I have been to Wind Cave, where the earth still breathes.

The Lakota recount in their version of demiurge, the creation story that the gods lived in the heavens and humans lived in an underworld without culture. Creation was initiated by Inktomi ("spider"), the trickster, who conspired to cause a rift in the heavens between the Sun God Takushkanshkan ("something that moves") and his wife, the Moon. Their separation marked the creation of time.

Some of Inktomi's co-conspirators were exiled to the Earth where the gods of the four winds were scattered and created space. To populate the Earth, Inktomi traveled to the underworld in the form of a wolf and met with humanity, telling them about a paradisiacal world aboveground. Inktomi convinced a man named Tokahe ("the first") to travel to the surface for a brief visit. When Tokahe emerged through a cave (Wind Cave in the Black Hills), he found the world to be strikingly beautiful. Returning to the underworld, Tokahe persuaded other families to accompany him to the surface, but upon arrival they discovered that the Earth was full of hardship. Inktomi had by this time prevented humanity from returning below ground, so the families had no choice but to scatter and eke out their livelihoods, populating the earth. They had emerged from the center of the breath of God.

All of the world's great religions and mythologies have at their basis a focus, or a center. For some it is chi, the center of power. Many times it is an historical figure: Jesus, Buddha, Mohammed, Abraham, Baha'u'llah (Baha'i), Moses, Krishna – all of whom *embodied* the beliefs of their followers.

We must find a center, which places us in the stream of not just humanity and human consciousness, but of human thought. It is there that we live and move and have our being. Prayer becomes the breath of human existence, and we too live within the breath of God.

We say that loving and being loved, hearing and being heard, touching and being touched, and reaching toward God with her reaching toward us, are the bridges we build to transcend the limitations of human existence. Our true future then lies not only within us, nor up in the sky somewhere, but all around us each and every day we still live and breathe. Losing ourselves ultimately leads to discovering ourselves. One energy state moves toward another, and nature in our lives is reaching for balance.

In our agony lies the condition of all humanity: a desperate cry for a response from others. We need others in order to die well. Our cry is not for religion, or even for forgiveness and salvation. It is the simple, yet indispensable and urgent cry for the tender embrace of another human being. In a novel, with a grace I cannot duplicate, Scott Turow says through one of his characters, "I am arrowed by the terrible humbling poignance of [this] simplest truth . . . In the marrow of the bone, where blood is made and beliefs are gathered, I'm hungry for the intimate company of other humans. I am lonely" (p. 388).

I pray that God will find me suffering proudly, not miserably, and in that I know how to die. If we do not learn the lessons taught us through suffering, we will instead be subject to bitterness and disillusionment, and find ourselves separated from the ones we love.

We have the choice to we turn our own suffering into triumph, Viktor Frankl says. "When we can no longer change a situation . . . we are challenged to change ourselves" (Frankl, p. 135). Once we accept such a challenge, our lives will possess meaning up to their final moments.

Rainer Maria Rilke, in his "Tenth Elegy" (Mitchell, p. 217), writes:

> How dear you will be to me then, you nights
> Of anguish. Why didn't I kneel more deeply to accept you,
> Inconsolable sisters, and, surrendering, lose
> Myself in your loosened hair. How we squander
> Our hours of pain.
> How we gaze beyond them in to the bitter duration
> To see if they have an end. Though they are
> Really seasons of us, our winter –
> Enduring foliage, ponds, meadows, our inborn landscape,
> Where birds and reed-dwelling creatures are at home.

When our grief becomes dear to us, when we deeply accept it, it leads us to contemplations far beyond ourselves, and can lead us to the face of God.

We have the choice to turn our own suffering into triumph, Viktor Frankl said, "When we can no longer change a situation . . . we are challenged to change ourselves" (Frankl, p. 135). Once we accept such a challenge, our lives will have meaning up to their final moments.

Part III: The Mystery and Holiness of the Present Moment

...when we finally know we are dying, and all other sentient beings
are dying with us, we start to have a burning, almost heartbreaking
sense of the fragility and preciousness of each moment and each
being, and from this can grow a deep, clear, limitless compassion for
all beings.

-- Sogyal Rinpoche

Our illnesses and the loneliness that so often accompany it are
actually gifts, which allow us – perhaps for the only time in our lives
– to look beyond the boundaries of our own existence. Too often, our
lives are built around the false presuppositions of health, immortality,
and a life free from pain. Shedding ourselves of these deceptions once
and for all is finally liberating. Adolescents believe that life will last
forever. As we become free of the notions of life-long good health,
and our lives free from pain, we are able to fully enjoy the moments
in which we live, and thus cross the threshold into moral adulthood.

Viktor Frankl said, " . . . everything can be taken from a man but one thing: the last of the human freedoms – to choose one's attitude in any given set of circumstances, to choose one's own way . . . It is this spiritual freedom – which cannot be taken away – that makes life meaningful and purposeful . . . The way in which a man accepts his fate and all the suffering it entails, the way in which he takes up his cross, gives him ample opportunity – even under the most difficult of circumstances – to add a deeper meaning to his life." (Frankl, p. 86,87)

You see, dying slowly, for those of us who are, is an experience which lies, I think, beyond explanations and investigations. Recording what others have said on the subject – and a number of books have attempted to do so – can never replace that experience. They can never truly describe it. No one honestly understands except each of us. And this is why I call it a gift. We have been given the unique opportunity to experience the inestimable beauty of life through the lens of our own personal suffering. Through that lens, we also begin to see a peace which truly surpasses understanding.

Death has no morals. The good still suffer. Evil men and women lead unmerited long and wealthy lives. Children die. It is as if life is out of our own control. In fact, life is. We want our lives, and our deaths, to come and go according to our plans and according to a script we have written. They never do. It is a costly mistake to live outside of truth, and death is the single, often apparently senseless, truth of living.

We cannot know pleasure in the absence of pain, joy without sorrow, peace without discord, or life without death. Our vain attempts to ignore one, enslaves us to both. The answer to these opposing forces is more than acceptance; rather it lies in fully embracing each. In surrender, we gain victory.

I spent a career entranced, watching the play of children. Their frequent desire to return to the same play activity time after time, week after week, reminds me that they are lost in a wondrous instant of joy, and oblivious to the passage of time. How much like them we must become! Lost in the wondrous, sometimes painful, beautiful, joyous, awful instant of a this moment in time! In that moment, in this moment, finally, there is freedom!

I have a five-year old client as I write this. He is an adorable child – my wife says I say that about all of them – with hair so blonde it is almost white, and bright blue eyes, with a shy smile lighting his clear and often glowing face. In our first session, he gravitated toward the doll house, with its small people and a multitude of furniture. He looked at me and said, "Do boys play with that?" I assured him that some did, and that he could whenever he chose to do. Week after week, he arranged the furniture carefully and neatly, placing dolls representing his father, himself, and his brother in the house, often side by side. He usually left out a mother doll. All was in perfect order. Yet in his home life, there was chaos. His mother had moved out, and his long-suffering father had undertaken the care of the boys, and was doing it well. In some sense, the child was lost in the artful activity of making sense of his world, at least in his play, when his "real" life was chaotic. Invariably, he left happy. I explained it all to his father, who told me quite simply that it makes the boy happy to be here, and for an hour a week the boy is able to just be himself. That, his father said, is enough. Would that more parents were so understanding.

Later, the same child began immersing a collection of animals in a container of water. I do not know what that means to him! I think he just likes watering the elephant, and bathing the tiger.

In an early Sunday morning radio sermon, I heard a man say, if you knew you had only one year to live, what would you change? If only one month? If only 24-hours, where would you be? As for me, I am using this time to be close to those I love. I want to be close to my wife, and touch the faces of my children and grand-children. I want to use more time holding the hands of friends, or hugging them in one of those "guy hugs", where your butt sticks out but your chest is allowed to touch. With some of my best friends though, we stand close, our cheeks touch, we wrap ourselves in each other's arms, and we whisper "I love you." Real men have no fears about being close to those they love.

We cannot spend our time; life is not a quantity measured in human terms. But I pray I make the most of this time for proximity and enjoying loving relationships in every way I can.

How would you use those hours? Hours are all we have. Or minutes. And I will say to those I love, "I want to be as sure as I can be that the waning light around me holds fast to your faces." Those of us who are dying live this truth one breath at a time.

Too often, our minds are so filled with time future, or past, that we miss this present, within which are held all of the mysteries of life. The Bible says, "All that hath been is now, and all that is yet to be hath already been" (Ecclesiastes 3:15). Both time future and time past are embraced in the present; yet by trying to regain the past, or to rely on a future which will not be, we are lost to the thrill and splendor of *this* instant.

I think we are all looking for freedom. We want to be free from the future and the past, we want to be free of agony, and we want to be free of guilt. I believe we search for these freedoms through our spiritual condition.

Daily we read about one religious group or another decrying the beliefs or practices of yet another. Frankly, I find it all terribly sad. How difficult can it be for religious groups of whatever stripe to see that we are all One, that our foundational beliefs are one belief, and God is one God? Through that spiritual connection, we all live and breathe, and have our beginning and end.

Our differences are far out-weighed by our similarities. Our core beliefs should lead to peace and unity. Peace and unity bring us to the truth of the world as a family. Our recognition of joining the earth family, both in living and in dying, is liberating. And, the route to our inclusion in the family is largely irrelevant. There is no singular way, no exclusionary path. Rather, there are many roads, all with the same core beliefs.

In his book, *Oneness: Great Principals Shared By All Religions*, Jeffrey Moses lists and briefly describes sixty-four principles shared by every major religion. He quotes from the writings of Judaism, Christianity, Hinduism, Buddhism, Confucianism, Islam,

Shintoism, Native American Spirituality, Sikhism, Baha'i, Taoism, Jainism, Sufism, and African Wisdom literature.

Each of those teaches, among other things, one God and a foundational principle we might call the Golden Rule: Do unto others as you would have them do unto you (Matthew 7:12). All say the soul is eternal. Importantly for me, in this wrestling match with dying, is the fact that all agree that there are many ways to finding the Divine Presence.

The Pawnee say, "All religions are but stepping stones to God." Christians are taught that "For as many are led by the spirit of God, they are the sons of God" (Romans 8:14). But perhaps the most moving for me is a Hindu scripture, paraphrased from the *Bhagavad Gita*, which reads:

> They worship other gods with faith,
> They adore but Me behind those forms;
> Many are the paths of men,
> But they all in the end come to Me.

The wonder of the mystery of dying lies in its companionship to the beauty of the present. Suddenly, when we come to embrace this truth, neither living nor dying are bound by space and time. We are truly free.

To *realize* means something like *to make real*. When we finally realize that the number of our breaths and the beats of our hearts are limited, we find the preciousness of each breath and each heart beat. Nothing then is irrelevant. Every second and its echo are prized beyond expression.

As persons who are dying, we seek to know that which cannot be known. We look for some structure, some logic, surrounding not just our final days, but our fading presence. Our faith may guide us in that, into the hands of a God whose name cannot be spoken, but whose presence can be known. But death has no structure; it has no logic.

It is our fear of finality which keeps us from the warm encircling arms of time itself. But that fear closes us off from the wonder to be found in our final days. The promise of the future no longer holds for us. The learning of the past no longer sustains us. Only the immediacy of this time exists, and that must be sufficient. Of a sudden, we realize that all things are small things, except the power, the presence, and the marvel of this incredible instance.

In our local paper this year, there was an article about three little boys enjoying the first warm day of spring. They colored the front step with sidewalk chalk, then collected the dust and dropped it on a daffodil to make it, they said, prettier. One commented offhandedly that he liked "gross things", so he planned a career as a surgeon. They kept a magnifying glass close by to look for bugs. All proclaimed their love of life – "We get to climb trees and color!" "We get to swim and play soccer and kick rocks!" "Besides a week off for spring, we should get 14,000 days off!"

With our dying, we may once again color with sidewalk chalk, and kick rocks. What joys! It helps to live knowing the end is closer to us, and that this heartbeat may be our last. There is a calculator on the Internet which will count heartbeats and your breaths from the day of your birth, or any other day, to today.

(www.health.discovery.com).

As of now, my heart has beat almost 2.5 billion times, and I have inhaled and exhaled over 500,000,000 breaths. How many have I missed? How many have I simply taken for granted? How many are there left to me? And how precious has each become?

The monk, poet and philosopher Thomas Merton wrote that the anxiety of human kind to avoid unavoidable death becomes more acute as our lives grow longer. A search – Merton called it a thirst – for survival in the future makes us incapable of living in the present.

Ours can never be a freedom from the situations in which we find ourselves; it is rather a freedom to choose both who we are and who, ultimately, we will have been within these conditions. We are able to choose both who we are, and who we will become in the next moments of our lives.

Within each condition we face, like some treasure buried in the tomb of a King, lies sleeping true meaning, in every, even tragic, moment of our remaining lives.

You see, it is not the accumulation of wealth, status, or "stuff" which determines finally who we are. These all pass away, or pass to the worry of those we leave behind with our dying breath. This idea alone can change our outlook toward the experience of dying.

Life is not in and of itself a possession. We cannot own it, store it, freeze it, or really even do much to maintain it. It is a fleeting thing at best, ephemeral at worst. All things rust and erode. In the end, we own nothing. Gathering, clutching for things will never bring happiness. As those who are dying, and finally aware of this as one more process in life, we are again the privileged ones. In our last

20

years, or months, or days, we come to realize that the human heart is all that really matters. Further, the reaching, and one hopes the meeting, of our hearts with the hearts of others in our lives is all that truly matters.

I was again in the Intensive Care Unit recently, where I learned yet another lesson about the process in which we find ourselves. The nurses in the ICU have only three patients each, and even that is occasionally too many for whom to provide such constant and gentle care. While my nurse changed an IV bag, checked my blood pressure, and more, soft music began to play from the overhead speakers. It was a small piece that perhaps everyone would recognize, Brahms "Lullaby". My nurse told me that the music played each time a baby was born. It is a lovely message.

Not long after my nurse left my room, across the nurse's station, I saw a family of perhaps ten people, and the chaplain, enter another room. Someone closed the curtains, and the door swung quietly shut. Now, the nurse's station is a busy place, and the professionals there work so well together, that the area is often filled with calm laughter and good natured conversation. But in a moment, the noise of their working and convivial tones fell silent, with a quiet that rolled like a shallow-water ground swell. Then, while the stillness surrounded us, the Brahms piece worked its way again through our rooms and our emotions. I asked later, and was told that when the family gathered with the chaplain around that woman's bed, her life support had been removed.

She died. And as she did, that placid wave rolled across the room, where all of those connected with it knew what it was, and when it happened, though none could explain it. But you see, as one soul was lifted to the heavens, another was born, screaming and crying. It was a precious moment.

How I wish that at the moment of our dying, some new soul will be born to carry the peace and love of living that has upheld me for so many years.

Part IV: The Stages of Dying We Will Experience

I announce the great individual, fluid as Nature, chaste, affectionate,
compassionate, and fully armed; I announce a life that shall be
copious, vehement, spiritual, bold; and I announce an end that shall
lightly and joyfully meet its translation
-- Walt Whitman

My wife reads our horoscopes to me almost daily. They are usually far from accurate, but when we choose the good ones, they tend to come true! It is foolishness to believe that the traveling of the planets will affect my daily life.

I don't think I could have ever predicted my own life. I don't think anyone can. We do not so much choose our lives or our careers, as they somehow choose us. Certainly, I did not choose to gasp for a last breath or two, with fluid from congestive heart failure filling my lungs. It just happens. But our lives are full of wonder when we watch for it. And in death, might we find an entirely new wonder? But then life is so predictable in other ways.

Before Kubler-Ross, the grieving process, both for us and for survivors, was thought to be this:

1. Shock/numbness;
2. Yearning/searching;
3. Disorganization/despair;
4. Reorganization (www.forbes.com).

I was shocked by my own diagnosis. I was also emotionally numb for a while. But when I began to connect with the reality of my situation, and allowed myself to express what I was really feeling, the numbness and shock left me. But Oh how I searched. Not only did I research my condition, but I also began searching for meaning in my life, and trying again to find connections with real people with whom I wanted to spend time. Yearning means "hunger", or "aching". Those I did, and still do. But my hunger and the ache I felt so deeply inside myself was for the love and acceptance of others in my life.

I'm not sure I ever slipped into a true disorganization in my life, nor did I experience true despair. A compassionate realism will not allow for despair. Read again in Viktor Frankl. Even in Auschwitz, he never despaired completely. But the reorganization of my own thinking, my own feelings, and my own actions, is an on-going task.

At one visit with the cardiothoracic folks, I was to undergo a battery of tests headed toward a heart transplant: electrocardiogram, echocardiogram, metabolic stress test, and right side catheterization. That last means they cut my jugular vein, insert a probe, and checked for blood flow and the presence of fluid in my heart and my lungs. It turns out my ejection fraction was the same, but they found no fluid,

24

and the blood flow was good. They said it would be at least six months before we would consider a transplant! Then I asked the team administrator this: You're telling me that if there are things I want to do, I should do them within the next year. She looked at me gently, and said yes. I continue to reorganize my thinking around all of that; and I'm already planning a motorcycle trip for this summer.

Years ago, Elizabeth Kubler-Ross wrote about the stages of death and dying, based on her own work with hospice patients, and having shared with them in their final months. None of us necessarily follow the process perfectly; we may spend more time in some stages than in others, and we may revisit some stages along the way. These, I think, hold fairly true for many of us:

1. *Denial.*

Think of the first thing we say when we hear of the death of someone we love: "Oh no!" As we are now the ones who are dying, our initial response was most likely to have been that it could not be so. Surely this was happening to someone else, but not to me. Yet, this time, it is I. Denial of my own diagnosis is futile.

2. *Bargaining.*

Bargaining is best illustrated by the whole idea of there being no atheists in foxholes. If God will just get me out of this mess, I'll become a minister, I'll donate my body to science, I'll never drink again, I'll, well, something. God does not interfere with the will of man or with the laws of nature. Our bargaining with him is meaningless.

3. *Anger.*

Anger, to my way of thinking, may be the stage of dying which all of us experience most intensely and perhaps for the longest periods of time, coming back to it again and again. Life is not fair. Heart failure, and cancer, are not fair. But they happen to us, and the reality of dying before we anticipated it makes us very, very angry. Unfortunately, I think we take this anger out inappropriately – on doctors, on our family, and on ourselves.

Psychologists tell us to learn to express our anger, and this is not bad as long as it is done in healthy ways. But I fear we have been forced somehow to trying to avoid *feeling* our anger. I cannot do this. I do feel it, and it is often intense. What I have done is to become fully aware of my anger, embracing it as my own, and then expressing it appropriately. Denying anger will just lead to more sickness. But anger does not last forever; it is fleeting. And as soon as it flees, I must let it go. Hanging on to it is sickness, and I am sick enough already!

4. Sadness.

We have every right to be sad. Our lives are being cut short of our expectations. We have so much left to do. I asked my mother to read an early draft of this book. When I next visited her apartment, before she said anything else, she took my face in her soft and wrinkled hands, and said simply, "I just cannot imagine my life or the world without you it." The thought of this world without us in it, the thought of *not being* in a literal sense, is cause for deep depression. We will one day cease to be; we will never *cease to have been.* In that, there is comfort.

5. Acceptance.

Be certain that acceptance of our own impending death is not acquiescence or

resignation. It is more allowing the reality of our life's end to become a part of our thinking and feeling, and being determined to die well.

It distresses me a little that Kubler-Ross was able to identify so clearly what I would feel, now that I am dying. I never wanted to be so predictable! Perhaps it disturbs me because in no way do her stages of death and dying represent the journey of my life. They represent only the last few years, or months, or days. Who speaks, or what speaks, for sixty years of living?

I have taken to reading obituaries in the last two years, partly because I have decided to write my own. I want to share one with you.

A man who was 84 years old died in 2006. His obituary described where he had lived, where he went to elementary and high school, and that he served in the U.S. Army during World War II. Now read this list carefully: he fought at Normandy, Brittany, the Loire Valley, Luxemburg, the Heurtgen Forrest, the Battle of the Bulge, at Rhine, Neuse, Over the Rhine, and in Central Germany over the Elbe to Zerbst. He taught high school English for 33 years, retired, had an active volunteer career, and sang the National Anthem at professional baseball games. Following these descriptions, there were fully nine column inches of relatives. The obituary noted he was also survived by a "host of nieces, nephews, and friends whom he loved dearly." The hero's obituary was an entire column long. The review for the new "Superman" movie was three times as long.

What stands behind our names in obituaries seems not to matter much, and yet it should. This man's column was a final testament in writing to what he had done. But the testament did not tell us who he was. It did not tell us of savagery and bravery at Normandy or the Battle of the Bulge. It did not tell us of being part of the invading force in Germany. It did not shine light in the dim corners of the life of what must have been a truly brave and wonderful man. The truth is this man's story, the real story of his life, includes both his incredible bravery and continues to be told in the column inches that affirm his connections with family and friends. Our stories are told in our lives and the magical connections we have made with others.

Ultimately, our stories are stories of love, and the bravery of living every day.

Viktor Frankl, in *Man's Search for Meaning*, says the stages of dying are three:

1. *Shock.*

In a state of shock, we begin to deal with the denial, and overwhelming electricity of the moment we learn our lives are suddenly very limited. Many of us consider suicide; most of us decide against it (Frankl, p. 26).

2. *Apathy and Injustice.*

After the shock has begun to subside, we all must deal with the injustice we feel about what is happening to us. It is beyond our control, and we feel as if our lives – what is left of them – are also out of control. For some, this leads to apathy. – not caring. We say to ourselves that since there is nothing we can do about it, then nothing at all matters (Frankl, p. 47).

I have a friend who recently planned a wonderful birthday party for his fiancée. He rented a tent for the back yard. He bought mountains of food. He had barbecue grills arranged. Then the rains came – torrential ones for three days before the party. His garage was flooded. His backyard was flooded. He called me in misery and said, "I'm never planning another party! It will rain every time I do!" Because it rained once, the rest of his life is destined to be flooded. His faulty logic, rather than actual weather patterns, would direct him to inaction, which he saw as dominating the rest of his life, was ridiculous.

Our apathy, if it comes, can cause us to squander the balance of our lives, no matter how great that balance may be. That would be tragic.

Frankl says that following the apathy, when we overcome it, lies an intensification of our spiritual lives. When we know our time is limited, we build, or rebuild, our relationship with a power greater than ourselves.

3. *Finding meaning in love.*

Frankl believes, and I agree, that as our spiritual life intensifies, we will experience a psychological state that can only be called liberating. Liberated from our outmoded and unnecessary focus on self, possession, and property, we are then free to love others unconditionally (Frankl, p. 55).

You can choose the pattern you want to guide you in the dying process. Personally, I'm following Frankl. I want to be liberated, and lose the focus on self that has guided most of my life. I want to lose a focus on possession, which sets me free from being owned by the things I own. And as certainly as the sun rose today, it will rise again the day after I have died. I want to be free to love unconditionally. Now.

Part V: The Meaning of Our Lives

Because I have loved life, I shall have no sorrow to die.

-- Amelia Burr

In order to give our lives meaning, in order to die well, we must enter the lives of the living. In very large part, the meaning in life arises from the meeting of individuals. And most often, in our meeting with others, we must enter with them into their fear of dying, and together share in the resurrecting from that darkness to light. When we are no longer alone, hope becomes possible in life and in death. When our suffering is shared, we find freedom.

Life becomes meaningless to those who close themselves off from the present or the future – however limited or unknown that future might be – and choose instead to re-enter their own history, their past, to the exclusion of all else. The Chinese character for crisis includes both the character for danger, and the character for opportunity. For me, this describes better than all else, the lot of humankind. Each day, each event, is a cause for both danger and for opportunity.

Frankl says that the search for meaning has been the primary motivation for his life. That search is unique and specific to each human being, and may only be fulfilled by each of us alone. We are able to live, and even die for our ideals and values.

We am not searching here for something abstract and mysterious about the *meaning of life* in general. I am not sure we care – or have the time – for such lofty ideas. Rather, I am searching for meaning in my life, here and now. And the meaning for your own life may be far different than mine. It depends on who you are, in your time, and in your unique set of circumstances.

It follows then that I am responsible not only for my life, but also for my life's meaning – and so are you! The meaning for our lives is to be discovered in the world around us, even more than in ourselves. You see, meaning is perhaps better found *without* than *within*, although we cannot begin to look outside ourselves until we are familiar with the inside. Our interiors may be difficult to slog through.

Certainly, some meaning for each of us may come from what we have accomplished. But I believe it is a more focused thing. We discover true meaning through experiencing others, and by the attitude we take to our own suffering. We experience goodness, truth, gentleness, and honor in the world around us. And we begin to know others by loving them and allowing ourselves to be loved unconditionally.

For each of us, life has meaning on at least two levels: at the level of individual moments, and at the level of those times as some sort of single mass. Our true meaning arises only at the end of our lives, which means that those of us who know we are dying have been given a very special gift: the ability to affect the moments we have yet to be given, and the ability to alter, if we must, the totality of our lives. We may choose, even today, what we may do with any given situation in our history, in our present, or in whatever brief future we may yet possess. Knowing this, we may alter the true meaning of our lives by its last moments.

We may know meaning in our lives by the things we have accomplished, although those things will fade quickly with the passing of time. We may find meaning in those we have loved, and perhaps most importantly in our case, by turning our suffering into triumph. The last is the triumph of our attitude – an attitude we may choose to the very end of our conscious days.

The establishment of our dignity is not founded on usefulness alone. In America, men – and more recently women – are too often judged by how "useful to society" they are, and by how much money they make. When we are no longer "producing", we may feel useless. But the true meaning of our lives is more honestly related to the dignity and value of every human life, than it is to our ability to produce a product of whatever kind.

In the end, our deaths are embedded in the meaning we ascribe to our lives. Virginia Woolf said, "What is the meaning of life? . . . The great revelation . . . never did come. Instead there were little daily miracles, illuminations, matches struck unexpectedly in the dark" (Woolf, Part III, Chapter 3).

Most people illuminate only events in their lives. Each of us, I believe, can be a soulful spark, illuminating however briefly the dark pocket of the corner of life we claim as our own. The true meaning of our lives lies not in any sort of revelation, but in daily miraculous instances brightening the ideas, thoughts, things, loves, places and persons, all of which may be lit however brightly by that flash.

However, meaning in our lives may be restricted by our view of ourselves. At first, my own impending death led to an emotional isolation. I did not want to light the lives of others. Life was unfair. I had worked so hard to get almost to the point of retirement, only to come to terms with the fact that I would probably not live long enough to collect my social security. Not wanting to hurt my wife, or my aged parents, or my children, I withheld information from them. I took numerous medications sporadically, continued smoking, and threw caution to the winds when it came to eating. Nothing mattered anymore. I still do not drink, but I took pain pills with reckless abandon. My view of myself at that time was that I must not matter very much, my life must have been largely without meaning, and therefore my family and the world at large would be better off without me. How horribly wrong!

At a recent outdoor concert, I had to rest to calm my rapidly beating heart while walking from the restroom back to our seats. I headed toward a bench to await a tram, and a handsome young volunteer asked me how I was doing. Normally, I would say "Pretty good today", or "Not bad". But that day I disclosed the full truth. He reached for me and touched me gently on the shoulder, guiding me toward a bench. In our conversation while I waited he said that he and his young wife – an opera singer – were going for ice cream after the concert. I told the two of them to eat a lot of ice cream. Do not look back over your life, lying on your death bed, and wish you had eaten more ice cream. Ice cream is a good thing. They promised they would.

There is a T-shirt popular among us motorcycle types that reads, "I refuse to tiptoe through life, only to arrive safely at death." Personally, I refuse to die muttering, "I wish I had . . ." I wish I had told you how much I love you. I wish I had held you one moment longer. I wish I had held your hand, but did not because I was afraid. I wish I had stopped for one more sunset, one more mountain or waterfall, one more sunrise. I wish I had touched the life of one more child. I wish I had reached through my fear into a life of richness and light. I wish I had eaten more ice cream.

Not long ago, I was taking a young man back 'home' to a treatment center for substance abuse. He is a fine youngster, who simply associated himself with others who introduced him to some deadly substances. I have known him for several years, though he is forty years younger than I. Always, I have treated him with tenderness and understanding. As we rode, in the dark, we fell into that silence that is often warm and comfortable between friends. Then quietly, he turned to me and softly said, "I love you Neil." There was nothing inappropriate in it; he said it more as a matter of fact. I asked him why though, and he said, "I think it's because you listen to me." How glad I am that I have been able, somehow, to touch that young life.

Let me tell you another. One summer I worked at a gas station in a National Park out west. A car pulled in one day, carrying a man and his wife, and a boy who looked to be about 14. The boy jumped out of the car while his father pumped the gas. The child ran immediately to the large out-door ice cream freezer we had near the door of the station, opened the lid to a cloud of steam as the freezing air met the heat of the day, and turning to his father he said, "Abba!" The man *immediately* turned toward the boy, and said, "Yes, my son!" *Abba* is Aramaic for "father", and is used in a filial, affectionate way, usually from a younger to an older person. It is also the term Jesus used when addressing God. I laughed, as I knew the term from my studies, and with the father's permission simply gave the child the ice cream of his choice from the cooler. We talked briefly, and I saw them several more times as they motored around the park.

One day about a week later, the same car pulled into the station. The father got out and came to me. "I am not sure why, but he wanted to see you." I walked to the car, the boy got out, and came to me. He said, a little embarrassed, "I just wanted to say good-bye." Then he put his young, thin arms around me, and hugged me close to himself. I touched his cheek, and ran my fingers through his dark curls, telling him simply to continue being himself. I've always wondered what that was all about, and wondered what happened to that boy. I would love to know. But in some mysterious way, I had again touched the life of a child, and it brings me to tears as I write this, over thirty years after the fact. It is also a little difficult to think that that curly haired, dark eyed boy is now over forty years old! Does he remember as I do? I hope so.

I suspect, at least I hope, there are many such moments in all of our lives.

Once I was in a tiny restaurant down a dark back street in Rio De Janeiro, Brazil. I loved Brazil. My friend and I were very hungry, but spoke no Portuguese. I asked for a menu in French, in English, and in Spanish, but could not make myself understood. Finally, I ambled around the restaurant, looked at what the locals were eating, pointed at a dish that looked inviting, and held up two fingers, then pointed at our table. Fortunately, the waiter understood instantly when I said "Beer". I have no idea what we ate, though it looked vaguely like beef, and it was delicious.

For those of us who are dying, we have no menu from which to choose, and we are unable to get others to understand us. Heart failure? Cancer? AIDS? Lung disease? We cannot, prior to the experience itself, make a choice. But we may make the experience itself a meaningful one, even if we may never describe it completely. Like the child in the story from the park, we may only keep on being ourselves.

The compassion we ask from others is really unsentimental. They cannot understand, as they are not (yet) in our position. We do not seek their sympathy, and they are incapable, regardless of their genuine attempts, of honest empathy – feeling the things we feel. They may say they know how we feel, but they do not. Compassion implies by definition oneness with suffering; our desire, really, is for others to simply be themselves for us, to be available emotionally, physically, and psychologically, and to sit in silence with us. Words alone cannot ever communicate what we feel, what we think, or who

– in this experience we call dying – we truly are at this particular moment in time.

An outgrowth of this need for relationship is the recovery of our wonder at the worlds in which we live. I have ridden touring motorcycles for most of my life. Having accumulated literally hundreds of thousands of miles riding, I have visited all 48 contiguous states in the United States and nine provinces in Canada on the seat of various motorcycles. Through all of those rides, my love for the wonder of the world and the joy of even the most casual roadside meetings with others have kept me fully alive to the beauty, motion, and the presence of God in all that I have seen.

Yet today, as I write this, my wife of 25 years climbed gingerly onto the back seat of my Harley Davidson. The fire-belching beast moved us into late spring 80-degree heat, through the magnificence of early planting in Ohio farm land, and into a closeness with her, a relationship in space and time and physical union that felt as if it was all somehow new. My heart was filled to overflowing with the joy, the wonder, and the warmth of it all. There can be no ownership in that; only the joy in each brief interval of time, and the sharing of those moments. I know, and she knows, that I am slowly dying. But today? Today we are fully alive.

My feeling is that just listening to those of us who are dying is perhaps too difficult. Perhaps we confront others more with their own deaths than ours. Perhaps our acceptance flics too clearly in the face of their fears. Perhaps our desire to learn from the process of dying is too great in light of their own tenacious hold on a finite world. Perhaps being with us in our pain is too powerful to be filtered through the preconceived mind-sets and notions of those who have yet to be given the gift of consciously awakening to life's final mystery.

On a recent motorcycle tour across Wyoming, I had engine trouble due to some bad gas. In a town with a population of 50, nestled in the windswept prairies of southern Wyoming, a man who owned a snowmobile dealership came with his trailer and took me and the shiny monstrosity back to his shop. While he worked on the motorcycle, I spent two hours talking with his wife, a round-faced, pleasant woman and former nurse. She held my hands, looked at my face, and dragged an oxygen bottle over to me, placing the tubing over my head and over my protests. "Your lips and fingernails are blue. Just use it!" In truth, it was more of a motherly command than a request, and I did as I was told!

Based on the blue fingernails, she asked about my health. While I fully expected the usual litany of pat responses, I nevertheless described my condition. "Hmmm," she responded, "how long?" I told her two or three more years, and she sighed. Then she told me she had leukemia, with an indeterminate prognosis. Her thought was that if I took care of myself (and stayed out of high altitudes) it could be longer. But during most of the conversation, I simply listened to her. Really listened, openly and honestly, without any preconditions or any preconceived ideas. When her husband finished with the motorcycle, she told me she was so glad she finally had someone to talk to about her disease who understood what it was like to face death on a daily basis. In both of our cases, all it took was someone to sincerely listen.

When we can stand with another human being just as we are, then our hearts reach their hearts at the very core of human perception. It was there that we two met. She hugged me when I left, and with my cheek dampened by her silent tears, she kissed me when she said goodbye.

The approach of my own death has led me to a greater sense of connection, not just with others, but also with this pulsing, vibrant, textured world. My sense of boundaries has become more inclusive, and any interference with that inclusion has become a challenge to be overcome. My compassion and love for humanity has grown. Property and financial security, much to my wife's occasional chagrin, have become much less significant priorities in my life.

The approach of my own death has led me to a greater sense of connection, not just with others, but also with the pulsing, vibrant, textured world at large. My sense of boundaries has become more all-inclusive, and any interference with that inclusion has become a challenge to be overcome. My love for others has grown, as has my compassion for all humanity. Property and financial security, much to my wife's occasional chagrin, have become much less significant priorities in my life.

Adam Smith observed that the chief part of human happiness arises from the consciousness of being beloved. The poet John Donne said that each of us is a part of the main. In Thailand during a Buddhist funeral, a string is tied to the cremated remains in an urn, and everyone present grasps that string. All are connected, not just to the deceased, but also to the others. We are all connected to each other, and each to life itself. When we come to know this truth, we

40

become one not just with each other in the beauty of human interaction, but with the brilliance and breathlessness of life itself. We are a part of the mystery, yet simultaneously aware of the mysterious.

Perhaps this is the perspective to which St. Paul refers when he says, "For now we see through a glass darkly, but then face to face" (I Corinthians 13:12). It is not in death that our vision clears, but in dying.

I once visited the power generating stations at Niagara Falls. The motors and generator were turning at near-fantastic speeds, producing loud whining sounds. As one was switched off, the generator slowed gradually, the noise decreasing as it did so. I assume it sometime later came to a complete stop, but it took a very long time, dropping revolutions only slowly, but surely. It was a lengthy process.

So is dying. We do not suddenly cease to exist. Our lives slow almost imperceptibly, but they may never come to a complete stop if we have found the true meaning of living, and of dying. Our contact with others, both intimately and with the world at large, have left ripples which extend far beyond ourselves. We do not "pass on" at a certain date or as the hand of a clock passes a particular mark in a sterile room. We do not cease to be. We enter a new phase of influence in the universe.

Unfortunately, words fail us when we try to describe the experiences of both our suffering and our knowledge of impending death, our deep knowledge of it. There are facts with which we may work: defibrillators, anti-immune deficiency drugs, levels of anesthetic and narcotics. But the knowledge, really the wisdom, of our process is beyond description. We are dealing not so much with facts, as we are with the impending and ultimate reality.

Staring straight at a star in the darkest of nights renders it invisible. Looking around it, peripherally, is the only way to see it clearly. Our lives have been burning and bright stars; but it is only in looking around them that we may see their truth, and know their place – their meaning.

Our deaths, like each of our lives, is much more a process than it is an end result. In dying, we are again the fortunate ones. We become able to see the process itself before the end result, which for us is the death of the body. Each of our lives is created, and in part I believe we create it, by a series of the tiniest decisions, each of which bears consequences.

But I still believe in miracles, events in real space and time that lie beyond the boundaries of sense and human understanding. Miracles imply the intervention of some power greater than ourselves in the lives of mortal men and women. And my belief in miracles encourages me to look beyond not only myself, but also beyond what I know in the physical world.

Indeed, I believe miracles abound in the world around us all the time. Einstein is quoted as having said that there are two ways to live: you can live as if nothing is a miracle, or you can live as if everything is a miracle. I choose the latter. In a way, they show us what was already before our eyes: almost everything is a miracle. Life itself, rocks, trees, flowers, those we love, love itself, are truly miraculous things and they are contacts in our lives. The Kingdom of God is within us and without us in every day of our lives. Those of us who are dying are privileged since we see this. Perhaps, in some small ways, we can share it with others.

I do not, however, believe in what is called the illusion of reprieve. Medicine is replete with cures which lie beyond any medical explanation. Yet all of us will die from our afflictions, some sooner and some later. This is not an effort to remove hope from our lives. Hope is alive, but for us it is a longing for a future which will not come. For us, there is no stay of execution, except perhaps for days or weeks. Even months.

Our deaths are not unlike our births. I remember when my first child was born. At that time, men were not allowed in the delivery room. But, immediately after she was born, the doctor brought her to me, still wet from the marvel of existence. I touched her gently on the cheek, her blue eyes opened, and she stuck her little tongue out at me. That moment, which brought me to tears, lives with me even now. That little one now has a Bachelor of Arts degree, two Masters' degrees, and she has just finished law school. Now that is miraculous!

You see, with her birth came the beginnings of limitless possibility and hope for the future. Those possibilities and that hope are real, and are still coming true. So often, I think, we see our death as some black hole, swallowing up the future and somehow negating our past. This is not so. Why is it that birth is an expression of limitless possibility, but death is seen as the opposite? It is not the opposite. When we die, aren't we again on the very edge of limitless possibility? The experience and its intensity are the same, and aware of our dying we are confronted with it.

We could not be consciously present at our birth. We are privileged to be truly present at our death. Others around us have become the children, observers of this astonishing passage. We are the miracle.

Part VI: Denial, Forgiveness, and Fear

Doubt, indulged and cherished, is in danger of becoming denial; but if honest, and bent on thorough investigation, it may soon lead to full establishment of the truth.
-- Ambrose Bierce

Forgiveness is the scent that the rose leaves on the heel that crushes it.
-- Anonymous

We need not fear life, because God is the Ruler of all and we need not fear death, because He shares immortality with us.

-- Ann Landers

What is denial? The fact of death closing in on us seems unreal. In fact it feels impossible not just to us, but also to others in our lives. During one of my own occasional but thankfully brief bouts of depression, I asked my cardiologist if perhaps he had misfiled my records, and the person he was treating was not I. When he assured me that he had not, I asked if he and the others on his staff were actually trained and qualified on the testing they had done with me. Surely it could not be me. But you see it *is* I.

In fact, it feels impossible not just to us, but also to others in our lives. I have been told that attitude about my impending death is somehow morbid, and that I "should not talk that way." Others simply refuse to acknowledge it, or in most cases refuse to discuss it. I am deeply moved by their love for me, and their denial is most likely an expression of that. But denial does no one any good whatsoever. They need it to protect themselves. Oddly, they think they are protecting me!

It is important for us to look closely at the issue of denial. Is it what is allowing you to function? Then by all means hang on to it, no matter how little good it does. Is it the only tool my friends and family can use to deal with me? Then they too should deny my death a little longer. Soon, they will have no choice but to accept it. But denial, theirs or mine, will change nothing. The price we must pay for loving and being loved is defenselessness to the pain of loss.

Most interesting for me, however, have been the reactions of others. You have heard them too, I suspect: "You never know what doctors will be able to do in two more years!" "Your positive outlook will add years to your life!" "Doctors don't know everything!" "It must be a mistake!" "I had an aunt/mother/father/brother/etc. with your diagnosis and they lived to 90!" "God will grant you a miracle, I'm sure." "I can't lose you." "What would I do without you?"

In all this time, no one has asked me how I feel. Not once. When others are confronted by the approaching death of someone they love, denial in some form seems to be the natural, and perhaps universal, response.

I suppose I was initially as much in denial about my own death as you are, or were, about yours. But thanks to the wonders of cyberspace, as I researched my condition on the Internet, my denial fairly quickly gave way to the cloudy dawn of acceptance. As I mentioned earlier, the two-year mortality rate for a heart condition such as mine is 85%. As I write this, it has been about three years since my diagnosis. Denial, for me, will serve no meaningful purpose. It would serve only to distance me from the true reality of my situation, to hinder my progress both in loving others and to a true acceptance of an impending fact and accepting a certain eventuality. That is energy that I choose not to squander.

It is not so much that we are hiding from life, as continuing to deny death. But then we just hide from ourselves the delight and splendor of life itself. Isn't our denial of death a vain attempt to interrupt or circumnavigate the cycle of life? This must not be.

In a battle between life and death, all of us will one day lose. Each of us will one day die. But death is not separate from life; it is a part of it, the two poles comprising a single whole. Pretending death does not exist, even resisting it for a lifetime, will not eliminate it. Again, surrender is the path to victory; nature is still reaching for a balance.

I believe there are people in our lives who wish we'd get on with it, or even get it over with. They do not really want us to die – at least most of them do not! But it forces them to come face to face with their own demise. Others, at the same time, cannot bear the thought of losing us. In both cases, their fear of our dying, and of their own death, has somehow caused us to be a terrible weight for our family and friends. It is emotionally exhausting for them, in part because our dying means a loss of control over their own lives. We are afraid of the things we cannot control.

Be certain of this: The only ones who can truly know what you are experiencing are others like you. Our spouses, partners, parents, children or friends cannot know. In truth, I do not believe that as hard as they might try, they can ever understand.

Our pain is our own. It sharpens our daily lives and is our constant companion. When others say, "How are you?" most often they do not really want to know. The truth is far too difficult for them. Usually, we bear this burden alone.

Our fears and doubts are our own as well. Imminent death has brought us to the shadowy edge of life. But the barrier between life and death is paper-thin, and a thing through which we see only dimly. Fear of dying, if we carry it, marks our attempts at some perception of the unknown. Even if we could verbalize our doubts and fears to those we love, I am not sure we would, or even really should. In my own life, perhaps one of my greatest current frustrations is that I must use so much of my waning energy to protect the ones I love from what I think and feel. They are trying to cope with the idea, a still cloudy one for them, of life without me. I am trying to cope with eternity.

Shadows happen when light is interrupted. But the shadows in our lives are really insubstantial. Our fear obscures love, anxiety our future, worry the glory of this day, depression the joy of the past. When we step through these invalid feelings, the shadows flee. Death is no longer evil or even destructive. Rather it is a simple fact of life and living, and one with which we must come to terms.

You see, we give people, places, things, ideas, and even emotions power in our lives. They do not hold it intrinsically. Presidents and dictators rule by the permission, explicit or implicit, of those they govern or oppress. Death rules so many lives because of the power we give to it, as if it is a thing, or a person, rather than a realm. Its power over us is determined by our fear and abdication to that fear. When we no longer fear death, it loses its power; only then may it become our ally.

Facing death compels us look at ourselves. Many of us grew up feeling we were somehow less than we were meant to be, or at the very least less than others around us. Out of that insecurity grew a need to please others, and in doing so we put on faces we thought others needed to see. For years, I used a portable electric razor in my car as I drove, so I never had to confront the face in the mirror. T. S. Eliot said we prepare "a face to meet the faces that we meet. Many of us do our best to avoid a confrontation between who we are, who we think we ought to be (or have been), or what _we_ think _others_ think we ought to be. This chameleon-like approach to living is no longer worthwhile, and certainly not valuable, in the face of death. It is life-denying.

As I approach my own death, I prepare no face except my own. The wonder of that has been the peace that has come with it. Dying with a face other than my own is unacceptable.

I hope I die peacefully. But I am fully prepared to be myself when it happens. If I am in pain, I will shout. If I am angry, I will rage. If I am overwhelmed at leaving those I love, I will cry. But my actions, my face, will be my own, and not what I think others think I must be. I will die as emotionally naked as I was born.

I was a breach baby, beginning my life backwards. Some of my friends might say I *still* approach the world that way! But, my mother says I was a quiet child from the beginning, almost never crying at all. Perhaps that is how I will end my life: quietly. I would like to think so. But in the same way I surrendered the comfort and warmth of the womb, I will surrender to the full humanity of my dying, whatever that entails. As surely ass the child I was surrendered the known for the unknown, so will the adult I have become let go of this life, unashamedly and honestly, for what is yet to come.

And, like you, I am guilty. We all are. I have a friend who says simply that everybody is guilty of something.

Guilt lives in the self-images of who we once were. We find forgiveness in who we are now. Our past is an artifact of what once was, and it is useless for us to permit who we once were to dominate who we are today. Having sought forgiveness from others where possible, and from God as we understand him, we can live today with a past washed clean. The word "repent" means literally to "turn your mind around." If we have turned our minds around from the actions, beliefs, values, prejudices, and mistakes of the past, and if we now live in a new direction, we can be free of the burdens of our past.

So often we are held hostage by our own history. A hostage has nowhere to turn, no way to grow, and no way of escape. We have become hostages to circumstances we cannot change – yet the person (us) in the center of those circumstances no longer exists. We are not today who we were then, because we have grown and continue to grow. Keeping a self-image shaped only by the past implies our past has its claws deeply embedded in us. But you see the old things have passed away. They, and in fact who we were then, have died. Losing that feeble, bloody, injured self-image means that who I am today can forgive who I was then, as well as forgive those who were in those circumstances with me.

I do not believe we forgive, or are forgiven, simply by ascribing to some antiquated and rigid moral or religious code. From the child-like purity still alive in every human heart, we allow others to fail, and to fail us. We acknowledge that we have failed, and failed others. And in each case, we raise up our dusty selves and the others in our lives, and move on wiser for remembering that purity and experiencing that forgiveness.

In the Lord's Prayer, we pray, "forgive us our debts as we forgive our debtors." I'm just not sure that is all-encompassing enough. In the Metta Sutta (the Scripture of Loving Kindness), there is a meditation for forgiveness. In it, we are asked to open our hearts, and first forgive ourselves for any wrongs we have committed. Then we are asked to forgive anyone who has ever treated us badly, offended us, or "sinned" against us. We must let go of those wrongs. Finally we are asked to send loving kindness to – to pray *for* – those who have injured us. We pray for our enemies, for those we dislike, for all beings in the universe, for all humans, animals, plants, one-celled organisms and any other unimaginable life forms, wishing them perfect joy. In this meditation, completed over and over time and time again, we may find freedom.

Earlier we considered being held hostage by our past. Many of us may be slaves to it. Once at an antique show, I ran across a set of what looked like shackles, the ones that chain a person's ankles together. I picked them up, curious, and when I held them in my hands, it was as if I held something electric. Immediately, I dropped them back on a pile of metal, and asked the dealer what they were. "Oh," he said, "just shackles. These were probably used at a slave auctions. They're not worth much."

They're not worth much. They held a man or woman from freedom, perhaps while their bodies were being oiled to increase a sale price. They dug painfully into the ankles of those who were forced to wear them – men, women, and children. They destined a human being to a life of toil and suffering in a country not his own. They removed a mother from her child, and a man from his family. They were a first step in the loss of language, religion, and culture.

But, the dealer said, they are not worth much.

I believe that as a symbol for a dreadful time in American history, they are beyond price. I believe their value is so great they should never be sold – again.

How does all of this relate to forgiveness? The Greek root for the word "forgiveness" means to set free, as in freeing a slave. Forgiveness can set us free from the resentment, anger, and pain we carry toward those in our past. It also means we can free ourselves. But as I live through my final days, what is it that shackles me to a painful past? I believe we must forgive those who have injured us, as

52

well as forgive ourselves for injury we have caused to others. Like so many things this too is a process.

On a sunny day in May, 1981, Pope John Paul II rode standing in an open convertible among 20,000 adoring men, women, and children when 23-year old Mehmet Ali Agca reached above the heads of other worshipers and shot the Pope three times. John Paul was severely wounded by the bullets in his stomach, left hand, and right arm. Fortunately, none of the bullets hit vital organs, and after a six-hour operation he survived. Agca was captured immediately and received a life sentence. But three days after the shooting Pope John Paul II freely, openly, and publicly forgave Agca and requested clemency for him. In time, the Italian president granted the clemency, and Agca was returned to his native Turkey where he went to prison for other crimes.

In 1983 John Paul privately visited Agca in prison for twenty minutes. When questioned about their conversation after the visit John Paul said, "What we talked about will have to remain a secret between him and me. I spoke to him as a brother whom I have pardoned, and who has my complete trust."

So tell me – does the suffering of your own youth sound louder than the crack of the bullet striking John Paul in the stomach? Do angry words from someone who is supposed to love you spin you as quickly as the bullets that hit his arm and hand? And can you forgive such painful injustice? Well, you are alive! You may have scars, but you survived. What then enslaves you to a tortured past? It is your failure to forgive which has you shackled.

My life and my injuries require no apology from those who hurt me. It is me approaching them in the prison into which they have truly placed themselves that sets me free. My prior pain then transforms into a present peace. I do not condone the painful acts of others. We still may seek justice where that is appropriate. We may never forget the injury, and we may choose to sever any relationship with the perpetrator. But I refuse to any longer relinquish the joy of my present peace to those who injured me. I believe forgiveness is an effort on my part to refuse to wallow about in my own slavery and suffering. John Paul forgave his would-be assassin for his own sake, as well as for Agca's. In that quiet twenty minutes alone together in a dark Italian prison, forgiveness set both of them free.

And what of myself? As I said, I am guilty. We all are, of something. I have, both knowingly and unknowingly, injured others. Some, I suspect, badly. How can I forgive myself? I am not so sure that I am able to view myself with the same love and compassion I now readily offer to others.

I read recently about an ancient punishment for murder. The guilty one had a corpse tied to his back, so that he had to carry it every day and every night. In time, as the corpse decomposed naturally, the killer would become infected with diseases and he too would die.

I need no longer carry the corpse of past transgressions. I need not wait for an incurable infection contracted from the burdens once tied tightly to my back. My guilt has punished me enough.

Sometimes it bothers me to think that those who live after me will feel some guilt at my death. It is not an unusual thing in the grief process through which many of them will slog their way. Some will feel guilty about simply continuing to live. This, I think, is especially true for parents who outlive their children. Unfortunately, some many may feel guilty for just having fun again. Some will be relieved my ordeal is finally over, and then feel guilty about the relief.

Let me offer some things to those who continue to live after I am gone. I pray you sense my spirit with you as you go about your day, and that any dreams you have of me will be peaceful. This should be so. Please do not worry yourself over things that happened – or didn't – because my entire life led me to the acceptance and contentment I now feel. If you feel moved to tell stories about me, just do it! Laugh at me, at my mistakes, at the way I drove, swerving all over the road amidst open gestures as I talked, at the way I could lose my glasses when they were perched on my head. Laugh about my motorcycle trips, and the way I let my grandchildren fix my hair with tons of hairspray and odd colors when they were toddlers. They loved it, and so did I.

Include me somehow in your holidays and special times. If you set a place for me at Thanksgiving, remember I do not like the dark meat, and there must be biscuits on the table! Cry if you feel the need, but laugh often. Thank God for a life well-lived, by a man who loved deeply and often, and who was well-loved. And never, ever doubt that God is a loving and compassionate God, who welcomes us back into her arms. Grieve for me if you must, but please do not allow your grief to overwhelm your love of life. I have been told that in the Byzantine Orthodox Church, there is a celebration forty days after the death of a loved one. Have a party!

When I learned to forgive myself, I used the same tools I learned in forgiving others. I refused to suffer any longer over the mistakes, actions, and inactions of my own past, and I resolved not to make the same stupid mistakes again. I did not condone my own past behaviors, nor try to rationalize them, and the punishment I have heaped upon myself is enough.

The program of Alcoholics Anonymous suggests we make amends for our injuries to others, except when doing so would cause greater injury. Where I could, I approached people one-on-one and asked for their forgiveness. Some offered it; some did not, but in either case my own conscience was clear. Some, I could not find, and these I submitted to my prayers. In a few cases, I could only make donations to causes important to the other, as the person had died.

I have tried, in the time left to me, to resolve some of the tension and inner-turmoil which comes from the juxtaposition of injury to others, and a need for forgiveness. I have sought out those I am afraid I have injured, and sought also their pardon. In every case, I wish I had done so sooner. Consistently, I have been captivated by the tender poignancy of these moments of grace, and by my own reactions. To one I had owed a not insignificant amount of money – for over twenty years. I called him, and he laughed! He laughed and told me to forget about it.

But I believe the emotional injuries we have inflicted on others are the most difficult to face, and the most difficult to heal. They are also the most emotionally rewarding when they have actually healed. And, the passage of long periods of time is irrelevant to that healing.   Before I was married, I had a loving and gentle relationship with a young man during a summer job between school years. It was almost a father-and-son relationship. When the summer ended, I left abruptly, perhaps coldly, certainly without regard enough for his feelings. I have carried the burden of guilt for that through years and years. It took two years of sporadic searching on the Internet, but I finally found an obscure reference to him several time zones away. I wrote to him, and asked him to call. He did, and when he did I explained the hurt I felt when that summer was over, and tearfully apologized for the heart-breaking hurt I had inflicted on him. At first the line went still, and then a tear laden voice, that sounded much like it did all those years ago, spoke to me softly, telling me that he understood, and that he wished we had made contact years ago. In fact, he said that he too had searched for me. The rest of my day was lost in reminiscence and the peaceful joy of having finally having righted a heartless wrong.

Finally, in order to make some of the amends complete, I worked at contributions to causes greater than myself. Now, I am free. And I remain willing to make face-to-face amends if the opportunity arises. Yet I still carry some lingering sort of unease.

The poet Dylan Thomas said, "I will not go gentle into that goodnight...rage, rage against the dying of the light!"

The poet Abigail Nussey wrote:

Fear of Dying

Don't tell me the time---
I don't want to know.

I'd throw my watch away

And the sun

Just to stop time---

Dear Physics, I know!

Such fear spawns futile hope.

I'm afraid to die.

Every moment marks me---

The patient violence of sunrays on a prune;

Every moment brings me---

Closer

To the End, when the spark of the mind goes out.

The body's sag serves as notice,

More telling than a clock---

Gravity tearing the minutes away,

Minutes less where I cannot

Write,

Think,

Do.

We need to fear death, to hate

To think of it. To throw away our calendars.

Thought and action and focus are stymied by

Organization, spreading oneself out, one task at a time.

Let your mind, not the clock, measure each brilliant

Stroke of life. And fear death. Fear death and don't
Go to the calendar for reassurance, seeing empty
Weeks staring blindly like generous grandmothers.
Know time like this: it will soon claim you.

And then defy it.

How can I defy such fear? And as I approach my own death, why am I unafraid?

The word "fear" is most commonly defined as the distress we feel in the expectation of danger or pain. In its earliest roots, it may be taken to mean something like "losing hold". A better definition for us might be more like dread, which means to experience great fear or to be in terror. Both words have root meanings of an anticipation of danger. Our deepest fear then may lie in our anticipation of the process of dying, and our trembling and lack of sight as we approach the unknown.

In discussions with others, some of whom are dying as we are, I have yet to discover anyone who wants to die in pain. We all wish to die peacefully, yet many of us will die painfully. I was told recently by a hospice care nurse that my own death will probably be either in an instant (I have a terrible fear of dying in public, with my head falling into the pasta with garlic sauce on the plate in front of me!) or I will simply go to sleep and not wake up. At least not wake up in this world.

I really don't like the prospect of either of these. I want a chance for last words and a last hug, and a last kiss on a tearful cheek.

Something melodramatic would perhaps be more my style! Unfortunately, I don't get to choose. For those opportunities I would be willing to suffer a few weeks. Then again, we never get to choose the nature or the length of our own suffering. For some, such suffering has been a constant companion for a lifetime. For some it arises out of a battered childhood and then the unspeakable injustice in a dying a painful death. For some it is a physical illness, which may have lasted a few months, to a few years, to a lifetime.

But, a painful death seems somehow appropriate. Birth was a struggle and an earth-shattering event, leaving safety for insecurity and total dependence. Life itself, for everyone I think, has been a struggle. Even the very wealthy and the very blessed suffer as we do. So, why should this last transition be any different? And isn't it equally valid, equally important, as potentially earth-shattering, as the other struggles of my life? It is. Besides, a morphine drip works wonders. I intend to take whatever pain medications my doctors will prescribe, but end my days as consciously as I can. And if we reach that point, there is no real possibility of addiction, is there?

In a sense, I think we must be soldiers heading for a battle so fierce that none of us will return alive. Before the first guns fire, we all know we will soon die.

The surety of death sharpens our senses to every sound, every shade of light and shadow, every motion or movement. It is perhaps only when we are about to die that many of us are finally fully alive. You see, when the battle rages around us, our personal defenses are sharp and our fear disappears. Separated from it, willing to examine and face it, fully aware of those with whom we share this journey, fear becomes nothing more than a wisp of smoke, dissipating in the breeze of new life.

About 25 years ago as I write this, I had the opportunity to visit Greece, Egypt and Israel on a tour with other seminary students. Because of the nature of our group, and the bargaining ability of our guides, we were able to visit some places normally unavailable to other tourists.

We entered what is thought to be the tomb of Jesus, and later stood reverently before the silver star marking the place of his birth. We toured the national museum in Athens and wondered at the marble representations of gods long forgotten. But probably most striking for me was our visit to Egypt.

In the basement of the museum in Cairo, there are mummies stacked along the walls. Glass cases are filled with ancient jewels and pottery. It is an amazing array of antiquity dating back perhaps 5000 years. Yet, nothing moved; the room was so silent the squeaking of our tennis shoes echoed off the tile floors.

The pharaohs of Egypt spent a lifetime preparing for their deaths; or better said in preparation of their tombs. They dug elaborate tombs in the sand, and built pyramids that rose above the earth, all to proclaim they had lived. Their fear, I believe, was at *not having been.* Early on, however, archeologists ran into a huge problem: As soon as they opened a sarcophagus – an elaborate casket – the bones inside turned to dust with the first breath of fresh air. All of a sudden, the pharaoh was no more. His history remained painted on the walls and his varied and usually fictional exploits adorned his tomb. But his attempt at immortality was futile. The poet Percy

Bysshe Shelley said it well, in a short poem that may refer to the Egyptian king Ramses II:

OZYMANDIAS

I met a traveler from an antique land
Who said: `Two vast and trunkless legs of stone
Stand in the desert. Near them, on the sand,
Half sunk, a shattered visage lies, whose frown,
And wrinkled lip, and sneer of cold command,
Tell that its sculptor well those passions read
Which yet survive, stamped on these lifeless things,
The hand that mocked them and the heart that fed.
And on the pedestal these words appear --
"My name is Ozymandias, king of kings:
Look on my works, ye Mighty, and despair!"
Nothing beside remains. Round the decay
Of that colossal wreck, boundless and bare
The lone and level sands stretch far away.'

Percy Bysshe Shelley
December 27, 1817

So often people are like this great, misguided King. The mansions and monuments so many try to build decay and implode with the passing of time. However, the connections we make to others, and through others, last far beyond ourselves.

I believe the most consistent fear for those of us who are dying is the fear of non-existence. Yet the world has existed and functioned for millions of years without me, and it will continue to do so long after I am gone. I am no more than a blink of the eye of God. But, there is more.

I am in my dining room as I write this, on an early fall morning. The only sounds are the ticking of the kitchen clock, and the rustle of pages as my wife reads this morning's paper. The day after my funeral, it will be the same. The clock will still be ticking. The wall paper will look the same. The dog will again be lazing on her back, as my wife absently scratches her belly. Life will continue without me. How then do I cope with a world that does not have me in it? How can I continue to live and not live simultaneously?

First of all, I have touched the lives of many people – some of whom I will never meet – and so have you. In often odd circumstances, my eyes have reached the eyes of others and, however briefly, our souls have touched. This has happened to you too, this immediate connection. This is no real mystery. It is not love at first sight; it is simply *real sight*, and it has its basis in neuroscience.

We all have in our brains what are called mirror neurons. (See: *Mirror Neurons and the Brain in the Vat [1-10-06]*; *Ramachandran, V.S. Also, see other references on this site: www.edge.org/3rd_culture/ramachandran06_index.html*). In a way, these mirror neurons allow us to actually connect brain-to-brain, not to just feel *for* someone else but to actually feel *with* them. Mirror neurons allow us to share the feelings of others *as if the feelings were our own*. The mirror neurons allow us to share body states, emotional states, and sensations directly, brain-to-brain, with others. These then become parts of us, and parts of the others. Because of mirror neurons, we may be one with others in our lives, without ever saying a word. And each of us will be changed, at a deep and molecular level, forever.

Years ago, I was standing on a corner, waiting for the "WALK" sign. Then a little hand, warm and soft, touched me and took my hand. The little girl's father was with her, and without looking she thought my hand was his. Gentle, affectionate and trusting, for just seconds, we had deeply connected. When she saw who I was, she dropped my hand, and hid behind her father's leg. But I wonder if she feels now about it as I do. I will never know. But I know we were there. No one can retrieve such moments, but no one can ever take them from us.

I am connected with my family – my wife, my biological family, my daughters and my grand-children. I will always be a part of their lives, and through them a part of others. And due to the job that chose me later in my life, I have had the privilege of touching the lives of others, connecting with the lives of many children at their most tender and vulnerable moments. I have chased monsters out of closets and from under beds. I have walked with children through the deaths and desertions and the abuse and the lovelessness of their parents. I have held little ones on my lap, their tears dampening my shoulder, as they found a spirit they could trust. Some have told me they would have died without me, including a gay 15-year old boy, and a young man who found his first teenage love hanging in her basement. Through them, as long as they live, as long as their children live, should they have any, and their children's children, I continue to live.

You must have a family of some description. The word "family" has been redefined in recent years, to include the loving circle within which we find ourselves, no longer being limited to simply biological connections. Through those families you will continue to live. The people we love the most are soldiers with us. Our connections with them help to destroy stress hormones, enhance our immune system, calm distress, and shine light into life's darkest abyss.

I also believe many of us de-value our work. We may say, "I am only a steel worker." But steel products are all over our homes: they are in our driveways, and in countless other places in our lives. We would be much poorer than we are without them,. Or, we may say, "I am only a mechanic." But without you we could not drive our cars to work and play, and maintain our adhesiveness in our own families. We may say, "I am only a teacher." This last one truly bothers me, when I hear it from men and women who have been privileged to interact with and share in and help to mold the minds of hundreds of children. No honest labor is without value. None. And through the labor of your hand and heart and mind, our lives are enriched. Before the gladiators began to fight, they would face the emperor and say, "We who are about to die salute you!" They were headed for a battle to certain death. We who are about to die salute you in your work– and thank you for the ways you have touched our lives every day of our lives.

Konosuke Matsushita said, "What we should fear is not so much death itself as being unprepared for the eventuality...To be prepared for death is to be prepared for living; to die well is to live well" (www.stnews.org/rlr-1328.htm). As soldiers engaged in the battle with life and death, we are in a struggle whose outcome is a foregone conclusion. Our primary defense to *not being* is to *be now* as completely as we can. We too must reach for a hand which promises to be gentle, affectionate and trustworthy. That hand may be the hand of God.

Part VII: The Search for Divine Presence

All religions begin with

the cry, "Help!"

-- William James

I believe that deep within each of us lies some conception of something divine. Unspoken, perhaps just beyond our ability to describe it, we know that life is more than simple science or the random combination of colliding atoms. We know that life is more than physical substance, "created out of nothing, meaning nothing, whirling on to a destiny of nothingness" (AA, p. 54). Life is much more than the "nothing" some describe.

In Shakespeare's *Macbeth*, the poet put it this way:

MACBETH:

Wherefore was that cry?

SEYTON:

The queen, my lord, is dead.

MACBETH:

She should have died hereafter;

There would have been a time for such a word.

To-morrow, and to-morrow, and to-morrow,

Creeps in this petty pace from day to day

To the last syllable of recorded time,

And all our yesterdays have lighted fools

The way to dusty death. Out, out, brief candle!

Life's but a walking shadow, a poor player

That struts and frets his hour upon the stage

And then is heard no more: it is a tale

Told by an idiot, full of sound and fury,

Signifying nothing.

What an incredibly dismal view of life and living; how empty of joy or appreciation. This "nothing" I cannot accept. In truth, I cannot face life, and certainly I cannot face my impending death, without my faith in a power greater than myself.

I believe this may be the hardest thing for many of us who are dying. Parts of us cries in the loneliness of the night about how cheated we feel, about the fact that life is unfair, and about how others who are apparently so much less deserving than we, are alive and faring so well. I sometimes still cry at the thought of dying, when I allow myself to face the darkness of it. I suspect you do too.

I believe our human resources, all of our visionary ability and emotional strength, fail us when we look into the depths of our personal night, into what St. John of the Cross called the dark night of the soul. The author Oscar Wilde said, "Suffering is one very long moment. We cannot divide it by seasons. We can only record its moods, and chronicle their return. With us time itself does not progress. It revolves. It seems to circle round one centre of pain." We are bound by such suffering, and I believe our absolute need is for some power greater than ourselves to help us live our final months. Our conditions, past the medical ones, are such that only spiritual experience and a connection with God will conquer them. To find such a power, and such a connection, we finally search within ourselves for the existence of a power which is totally beyond ourselves. But how?

First, hear this: God is too great, too all-encompassing, to be enclosed in one small religious container. The spiritual universe itself is large enough for all humanity; it is large enough for all who seek it. Our path as we begin to walk toward a power greater than ourselves is merely a willingness to find that connection, or that presence. What others think, what brand of religion they may claim as their own, is of no consequence to us. We need a way to get through not just our futures however foreshortened they may be, but to just get through the day. I am sure about that religious container idea. All of the world's religions posit the concept of a single, divine, omnipotent or all-powerful God.

The Sikhs' varied names for God include One Creator, One True Name, Wonderful Lord, Destroyer of Fear, Dispeller of Pain, and Preserver of the World. Their scripture begins, "One God. Truth is His name. Creative being personified. No fear. No malice. Image of the undying. Beyond birth." Sikhs do not recognize God as being of either sex and the name of God is written without gender. English translations substitute male pronouns for the gender-free pronouns found in other languages. The Baha'i believe the essence of God is beyond the knowledge and the understanding of human beings. They say he may only be known by his attributes or through his names.

The Christian designations for God do not differ much from the world's other great religions. Based on what they call the Trinity, Christians name God as Jehovah, Jesus, the Comforter, Deus (Latin), and Father/Son/Holy Spirit. A further search finds the Christian supreme being called Bog (Slavic), The Light (Quakers), Haeland (healer in Anglo-Saxon), Iesus (Jehovah heals or saves, in Hebrew). In Islam, God is Allah, and is known by "the 99 names" or attributes. In their tradition, there is a one hundredth name, but it is not known, or if known cannot be spoken.

My personal choice – and clearly we have a choice since the names all seem to mean the same thing – is in Hebrew. In the Jewish tradition, the original name for God was YHVH (or YHWH). This is called the Tetragrammaton (four letters), and since in the beginning it had no vowels it could not be pronounced. I like that. God is so immense his name cannot be spoken. In fact his name becomes a sigh, or a whirlwind from deep within the human soul.

Most importantly for our purposes is that we all must have some sense of a power greater than ourselves. What we call that power is largely irrelevant. It may be only a deep feeling, lying just beyond expression. It may be the power you feel in a group held

70

together primarily by the members' love and care for each other. It may be God known by any of the names or attributes we imagine him to possess. But, I think the question remains, how do we find that power?   One summer in what was perhaps one of the turning points of my spiritual life, I met an Episcopal priest in Colorado one summer. Father H. Baxter Liebler had left his pampering and wealthy East coast home, traveling by train and then by horse, until he came to a place where people had never heard of Jesus. He spent the rest of his life in the West, working primarily with the Navajo. Father Liebler believed deeply in the conversion experience, but the Native Americans had no word for such a thing. The closest they could come was a term describing recharging a battery. They called it 'boiling the heart', and their request to the priest was "Boil my heart for me." Father Liebler authored a book by the same title.

This I believe is what we seek when searching for a power greater than ourselves. We want someone, or something, in some way, to boil our hearts for us. Fr. Liebler provided an avenue to that boiling through the Gospels, but his approach leaned toward what we might call the *authentic* Gospel. He offered the truly essential teachings of Jesus, which evolve from a sense of presence and openness. God is present in every moment of time, and if we are open to finding him, we will enter that presence with him. How?

A friend of mine asked me not so long ago how it was that I could maintain anything like serenity and peace in the face not just of my dying diagnosis, but in the face of the world at large. I explained to him it lay in my own relationship with a power greater than myself. Then he asked me how to find that power. My response was that we must empty our mind of all preconceptions of God or gods, empty our heart of all prejudice and resentment and rancor, and close our eyes to shut out, how ever briefly, the world around us, and reach our open arms to God. In this state of true emptiness, we will be alive in the present, open to the love which lies beyond human understanding, and God will fill the vacuum in our hearts and minds with herself. Here then we discover the existence of that power greater than ourselves, deeply alive within us, yet entirely beyond us.

A young man I had only known as sullen, depressed, angry, and distant from others, approached me recently. His eyes were literally sparkling, he walked with a new grace and ease of step, his shoulders were back, and his head was held high. "You're different," I said. "What happened?" He told me he had finally found a power greater than himself, and that he felt freer than ever. I asked him how he did it, and his response was that he simply stopped looking so much at himself, and began to look at others, and look for God. As time passed, he found both those in the world around him, and a new connection with God.

I think this youngster found at least two keys to a power greater than himself: he quit selfishness, and sought a relationship or connection with God. He opened himself, really, but I also believe that God – however you define him or her – wants to be a part of our lives. We must never doubt the drawing power that the spirit of the universe has for each of us.

Part VIII: Being Fully Alive, Letting Go, and Planning for the Future

An authentic life is the most personal form of worship.

Every day, life has become a prayer.

-- Sarah Ben Breathnach

Does it sound a little odd to talk about being fully alive, when each day draws us measurably closer to death? It is not, you know. How I wish I had learned these lessons years ago.

I've said it before, but will repeat here that my life has been – is – a good one. I have loved and been loved completely. I have ached terribly over mistakes and broken relationships. I have seen much of the world, experiencing its warm texture amongst the people I've met, and not all in high-rise hotels. They were often on the waterfronts, in small smoky restaurants, at family gatherings where bright dark eyes welcomed me, and in languages I barely spoke. I have sat quietly with Native Americans and others I've loved, high among the mesas of the

American southwest, and climbed to the top of the world in the Rocky Mountains.

I have listened almost in worship to the sound of a million polished stones, rustled and honed by the sea, tumbling in the waves on the coast of Brazil, and clambered up Dunn's River Falls in Jamaica before the tourists discovered it. I have snorkeled the crystal pools of the Florida Keys, catching lobsters in a pillow case, and grilling them on the beach as the sun began to sink so slowly we could almost hear it sizzle in the sea.

My life has been enriched by great books and a fine education, giving me the perspective I would otherwise never have had. And, I have been able to string some words together in ways that have brought pleasure to others.

I have been privileged to worship in great cathedrals; I've been awed by the reverence shown by thousands of people before me, their feet having worn waves in granite entry ways, dipping my fingers in water made holy by the love and reverence of centuries. I have prayed in magnificent Muslim mosques, run my hands through the waters of the Jordan River, and left a scribbled prayer in the Wailing Wall in Jerusalem. And I have known the filling spirit of small country churches.

But most of all, most importantly, my life has been filled with love. My family has loved and supported me throughout my life – though I suspect they didn't like me very much from time to time. I was somehow so often lost in my own mind and believing that they didn't understand. Many times, neither did I!

I have known the love of men and women, whose arms and hearts were, and are, open to me. I know today the love of men who hold me when I need it. I know today the love of one woman without whom my life would be less than half a life. For these I will always be grateful.

Oh, but I have missed so much.

This last fall I spent a wonderful day with my wife, walking as much as I was able, through a 9000-acre set of plantations in South Carolina. Years ago they had been rice plantations, worked by slaves. My poor wife trudged beside as I tromped along a path on a tripod of two unsteady legs and one cane. She was like one of those Buddhist monks who sweep the path in front of themselves to avoid killing even the smallest things. "Watch that rock!" she would say! "The sidewalk changes here pay attention!" "Don't bend over – I'll get it!" "Pay attention Neil!" God has blessed me with her love and care.

The thoughts I've just tried to describe went through my mind that day, threading before me and receding after me, as I allowed myself to be seduced by the warm, moist, simple wonder of the gardens. At one point I stopped dead in my tracks. (Maybe in a book such as this, that is not the best way to say it!) At the point of a small tilled part of a garden, a bright yellow flower had poked its proud little head above the mulch-blackened earth. It was brilliant, seeming almost to illuminate the space around it.

This is it! This is what I have been trying to say, to describe, to try to illuminate what Joseph Campbell called "the rapture of being fully alive!" Would that we all, beginning right this moment, right now, could celebrate that brilliance, that blessedness, the flash of eye-burning flame in the world around us!

The Unitarian Universalist minister Paul Beattie I think understood this joy:

When My Mind is Still

When my mind is still and alone with the beating of
my heart,
I remember things too easily forgotten:
The purity of early love,
The maturity of unselfish love that asks --
desires -- nothing but another's good,
The idealism that has persisted through all the tempest
of life.

When my mind is still and alone with the beating of
my heart,
I can find a quiet assurance, an inner peace, in the core
of my being.
It can face the doubt, the loneliness, the anxiety,
Can accept these harsh realities and can even grow
Because of these challenges to my essential being.

When my mind is still and alone with the beating of
my heart,
I can sense my basic humanity,
And then I know that all men and women are my

brothers and sisters.

Nothing but my own fear and distrust can separate me from the love of friends.

If I can trust others, accept them, enjoy them,

Then my life shall surely be richer and more full.

If I can accept others, this will help them to be more truly themselves,

And they will be more able to accept me.

When my mind is still and alone with the beating of my heart,

I know how much life has given me:

The history of the race, friends and family,

The opportunity to work, the chance to build myself.

Then wells within me the urge to live more abundantly,

With greater trust and joy,

With more profound seriousness and earnest service,

And yet more calmly at the heart of life.

> Paul H. Beattie, "When My Mind is Still," *The Community News*, [October 16, 1983], P. 3

You see, an authentic life is one which brings joy to others and a smile to your face, just at the magic of being alive. It is acting responsibly but spontaneously to even the smallest events in day to day living. If you're in a hospital as you read this, you've got flowers.

If you can't get it yourself, have someone give you just <u>one</u> of the flowers, hold it up to the sunlight, or against the whiteness of the sheet on which you lie. Look at it. Just really look at it, let its image sear itself in your mind, savor the colors, look at the turn of leaves and the curl of petals. Pay undivided attention to the flower, just the flower. And watch its brilliance fill the room.

But I cannot be fully alive, I cannot experience the rapture of being fully alive, if I have yet to let go of the people, places, and things which tie me to misery, worry, anxiety, and a world which is too burdensome for me to carry. I do not need to carry it, you know; and neither do you.

What happens if I do not learn to let go? If I cannot release my fears and worries to a power greater than myself, I will never learn personal serenity and peace. In fact, I believe this serenity and peace are necessary to relieving even our physical pain as our diseases progress. Without letting go and handing over our troubles to God, we will never be at rest. Right now, I long for rest, a rest deep in my soul which aches as I seek it. Finally, I think not letting go leads to depression (I have had enough of that already as I deal with my illness.) and engenders in me a deep sense of failure. But, if God is in control, I cannot fail, and he doesn't.

And how do we let go of such deeply entrenched attitudes, emotions, fears, and resentments?   The first step in such a process is a fairly easy one: There is only one thing I am sure of regarding God: I am not Him. Since this is so, I am not in any way responsible for things I cannot change. Remember the Reinhold Niebuhr's Serenity Prayer: "God grant me the serenity to accept the things I cannot change, the courage to change the things I can, and the wisdom to know the difference." It is neither my responsibility nor my obligation to change the things over which I exercise no power, no control, and no authority. Give it up and let God do it.

I believe many of us are bound up tightly in a sort of obsessive-compulsive relationship with the world around us. We think endlessly about a certain thing, and then act on that thought as if the whole situation is under our control. It is not. I do not have to be the perfectionist, who corrects every wrong, and straightens every picture! I must be more thoughtful about what I can do and what I can't. As time passes, there may be fewer and fewer things I am able to do, and I must give up my need to be the one who tries to do everything.

One of the best, if not the only, ways to do that, is to learn to say "No!" and mean it. When things are truly out of my reach, I must let others pick them up for me. On some level, I suppose I am admitting my own powerlessness over so many things in the world around me. To live successfully, to be fully alive, I must give those things over to a power higher than I.

I must become willing to admit my faith in a God who is more powerful than I, more able to manage the world than I, and the source of a power much greater than I. Since these things are true, I can give my troubles, my worries and frustrations, my inadequacies and pain, over to her. God is good; he is merciful; and he wants to shower me with his grace – with his goodness and kindness, mercy, and forgiveness. The solutions for my problems rest in her power, her wisdom, and her presence in my life. I must only surrender to God, in order to access this great strength. I surrender to God on a daily basis, and sometimes many times a day. I make it known, to myself and to others, that God is in charge of my life, my health, and my future, and that I am not. These things will allow me to let go of old hurts, old passions, old transgressions, and old worries. I need no longer carry them, as the convicted man does his corpse. When I stopped to simply appreciate that yellow flower, and when I learned that I am connected to the universe of the flower, as well as the universe of other loving persons in my life, I began living the rapture of being fully alive.

When we allow ourselves to suspend our judgment of other people, when we let loose of worry, when we become comfortable with the embrace of the love of others, we are beginning to experience the rapture of being fully alive. And when the yellow flower is truly a part of my life, I can plan for my future.

I suppose it sounds a little peculiar to talk about planning for the future when many of us don't have much of one left. It is not peculiar at all. It is hopeful.

I think the first thing we all must learn is how to remove ourselves from the flow of the hands on a clock, and experience each moment as if it were the only moment in history. In a way, it is. This moment is the only one that truly exists. The past is beyond retrieval except in memory, and the future is really just imagination. You see, you are planning for the future right now. You are planning to finish this page – or not. You are planning a warm shower, or sitting on the patio this afternoon, or looking ahead even further to school or a meeting with someone you love. But you are experiencing those future events in this moment in time. Doesn't that make this moment timeless?

The person we were before this moment, no longer exists. So you see, all of the important things in our lives, the things that really matter, are focused on this moment. This moment is our future! And in it we are complete.

No matter how sick you are today, you may still plan for the future – no, better said, you *must* plan for the future. Plan now to tell your wife or husband or partner that you love them. Plan now to hold your grandchild on your lap. Plan now to finish those small tasks that linger in your life and here I do not mean "work" as much as I do the emotional tasks that may be accomplished in the time left to you.

For the sake of those who care about us, I think there are some very practical plans we should make:

1. Update your will.
2. Secure a durable power of attorney.
3. Arrange for end of life decisions to be made on your behalf by someone you trust, including a "Do Not Resuscitate" order, if that is your wish.
4. Be sure there will be no financial surprises for those you leave behind, and that you can leave your life's partner as secure as possible.
5. Consider signing an organ donation document, so that others may live.
6. Write your own obituary and share it with those you care about, if you wish.
7. Have a party now, if that is your style!

8. Make your own funeral arrangements, stating exactly what you want: music, officials, type and order of ceremony if any, burial or cremation. Go so far as to choose your own casket, if you want one, in order to keep others from spending too much money on one.

9. Many people have some things tucked away in the backs of drawers that they do not really want others to find. Get rid of that stuff now!

10. Be certain that someone knows where all of your important papers are, such as insurance and funeral arrangements.

11. I have already contacted the funeral home of my choice, and begun paying on the arrangements; I don't want much, but I still want it my way.

12. A growing problem in middle- and high-schools is found among children who go to the homes of grandparents who have recently died, and steal remaining powerful prescription medicines. Designate someone to destroy any you may leave behind.

These things accomplished will make our passing much easier on those we leave behind. Is it morbid to discuss such things? Absolutely not. It is foolishness not to do so and an act of denial if we avoid settling them while we still can.

Part IX: The Summing Up

The life I touch for good or ill will touch another life,
and that in turn another, until who knows where the trembling stops
or in what far place my touch will be felt.
-- Frederick Beuchner

I think I intended this to be something between a personal reflection and a poem, aimed squarely at both your heart and my own. I hope I have accomplished some of that.

What have I learned in writing this for you? First of all, my motives were partly selfish: I had to figure out how I would manage not just a dire diagnosis, but also my own death. I needed to look it fully in the eye, and learn to approach it with courage. In this, I have succeeded. A professor of mine once told me that the novelist Virginia Woolf, in one of her diaries, said that we gain a kind of a hold on reality by writing it down. My writing this has accomplished that, at least for me. Perhaps reading it will do the same for you.

I went through a period of apathy and pretty severe depression for a while. I thought I covered it well, but according to my wife I did not. The depression still washes over me from time to time, but I am no longer apathetic. In fact, I care more about life and living than I did at the outset of all of this. My sense of spirituality is much broader and accepting now, and with the intensification of my spiritual life has come the liberating power of unconditional love.

You see, the presence of death in no way implies the absence of God. In fact, I believe we are closer to her if we relax and let things go. God is with me in my nightmares, in hospital waiting rooms, and soon in spaces I can only imagine. The Book of Psalms teaches us:

Psalm 139

If I ascend to heaven, thou art there;
If I make my bed in hell, behold, thou art there
If I take the wings of the morning or
If I dwell in the uttermost parts of the sea
Even there thy hand will lead me,
And thy right hand will hold me.

Ours is a God we carry with us in every moment of our lives, if we surrender to him. And when we die, when we take the wings of the morning, he will lead us, and his great right hand will hold us.

When I reached the point of no longer fearing death, it lost its power over me. It became my ally in my liberated approach to living and loving those around me. And we very much need others in order to die well.

Poor Will Shakespeare made Macbeth say that life was no more than a walking shadow, a tale told by an idiot, signifying nothing. He's very wrong, you know. The tale that is my life is beyond price in its telling. I am no shadow; I am truly substance, walking in bright sunlight and from me radiate love and laughter and a life lived to its fullest. This is no work for an idiot, nor as Bette Davis said, for a sissy. It is the work of angels. My life, my substance, will continue long after I am gone.

In 1953, Ray Bradbury wrote a short story called "A Sound of Thunder." In it, time travel becomes possible, but the repercussions are horrific. In truth, if a blade of grass is crushed, insects may die, which can lead ultimately to populations changing a thousand years later. It makes for fun reading. On a systemic level, if a butterfly flaps its wings in South America, it can theoretically have an effect on a tornado in Texas. The weather change idea arose from scientific symposia by Edward Lorenz in 1963.

For us, there is a lifetime butterfly effect. Our lives are not without meaning, and cannot be so, even if we wished that to be true. Having lived, however briefly, every action we have ever made, every relationship we have ever had, every love we have ever loved, will change the course of human history. Perhaps only in small ways, but then the flapping of the butterfly wings can cause a tornado in Texas. Your reading this short book, and my having written it, in small ways, change the course of human history. I do. You do. You and I together do. In this, we are one.

I have come to believe that I do not, can not, speak the name of YHWH. I may only find her deep within me, and make my prayer a loving sigh or a longing toward heaven. From that there comes an inspiration of love and hope. We too live within the breath of God.

Perhaps the true gift of dying is a sense of how fragile and precious each being and each moment are – and out of that realization grows a deep, clear and limitless compassion for all beings. We may look beyond our own existence. Within this compassion I am included, and I may choose my attitude in any situation.

This writing became a sort of cleansing for something deep within me. With it, I became able to objectify my own history, to weigh the good and bad, and to find those problems which still must be addressed. I've also been able to look back over 60 years and re-live some warm and wonderful times – but that is perhaps another book!

I think we must be able to identify the moments of grace in our lives. Grace is God's loving kindness as he leans toward us. In a book of poems titled "The Marriage of Heaven and Hell", William Blake said, "If the doors of perception were cleansed every thing would appear to us as it is, infinite. For man has closed himself up, till he sees all things through narrow chinks of his cavern." I think my most cleansing vision was the yellow flower. As I looked at it then, and watch it still somewhere deep within myself, I touch the infinity of the present moment, and find myself unconditionally connected to all of human history. As Paul Beattie said, "When my mind is still and alone with the beating of my heart, I remember things too easily forgotten." I choose not to forget. And I urge you to find the flower in your own life.

Through it all, I'm agreeing with Viktor Frankl. I can choose who I am today, I can choose how to respond to my own condition, and my own life, and by doing so, I choose who I will have been when I die.

Requiescat in pace

Part X: Epilogue

SEVEN YEARS LATER

It has been an eventful four years since I first wrote this little book. All of the copies I had privately printed have been sold or given to those in need of some comfort in their own process, or that of others. Many have told me it brought them peace. I hope it has done so for you.

First of all, I guess it is clear that I am not dead. I expected to be by now. My doctors told me my chances were slim for living even two years, much less seven. Even that is a little bit of a funny story, if we can find humor in such things.

It is the echocardiogram which allows the measurement of ejection fraction, which I explained in the early pages. Mine was at 15% seven years ago, which is deadly. It has since settled *up*, for the last year, at 35%. Second, there is a brain chemical called B-type natriuretic peptide (BNP), which is a hormone secreted mainly by the heart ventricles. While I do not claim a complete understanding of it, it is below a level of 100 in normals. At the time of my diagnosis, mine was at 1200; that too is deadly, though the BNP levels in some heart failure patients is considerably higher. It has since settled at 106 by last measurement, which is a pretty amazing drop.

On a visit to my cardiologist, whom I like very much, I told him my BNP was down to almost normal, and my ejection fraction had risen to 35%. I asked him why. He said, "Well, Neil, I don't know." I was a little concerned that my heart doctor didn't know why I was getting better!

What he said was that I am medically 'well compensated' right now, which means I am on appropriate dosages of the 14 medications I take daily. He also noted my weight loss, my continued efforts at as much activity as I can tolerate, and especially my positive attitude. Those, coupled with several rounds of other hospital treatments all contributed to the improvement in my physical condition.

I do not suppose in any way that others of us with terminal conditions can report the same success that I have experienced, and my heart is with you in your suffering. But, if the things I tried so laboriously to emphasize in these few pages have made any difference, you have come to realize the wonder of this moment in time, and the treasure we may find in the lives and persons around us, no matter how much time we may have left to us.

My long-suffering wife continues to tolerate me – somehow. Last year, over her protests, I rode my motorcycle from Ohio to visit my two brothers in San Antonio, Texas – in the summer. This, clearly, was a mistake. For two weeks, the temperature never got below 100 degrees, and my poor heart protested at the dawn of every day. I finally reached a point where I was stopping about every twenty-five miles to cool off. A particular coffee shop chain's iced coffee stock was sorely depleted for those two weeks! But along the way, I visited my 85-year old uncle for Father's Day, took my nephew for a 100-mile ride in the Georgia mountains, and traveled along the coasts of Florida, Alabama, Mississippi and Louisiana – where at one point a highway worker told me to watch out for the alligators that liked to sun themselves on the road in the afternoon. I'd never had an alligator warning before!

Let me tell you a story as I recall it, to go with this day in your life, no matter what your condition is. The story goes that some disciples of Lord Buddha were discussing him one day, when one of them approached him as he meditated.

"Lord Buddha," he said, "we must know – are you a god?"

"No," Buddha answered, "I am not a god."

"Are you a saint," the disciple continued?

"No," Buddha said, "I am not a saint."

"Well then," the disciple said, "are you a prophet?"

"No," Buddha answered, "I am not a prophet."

"Lord Buddha," the disciple said, completely confused, "what then *are* you?"

Buddha answered softly, "I am awake!"

I love that story, regardless of its authenticity. I am awake! On that entire trip to Texas and back home again, a distance of about 3800 miles, I was awake! Watching for alligators, I was awake. Through the cool shade of the Appalachian Mountains, I was awake. When my nephew held me tightly in a good-bye hug, his stubbled cheek pressed close to mine, I was awake. Through the ocean scented air of west coastal Florida, and into the heat of Alabama, I was awake. Eating deep-fried shrimp and deep fried pickles in Mississippi, I was awake. Over beignets and chicory coffee off Jackson Square, with trumpets blaring and fortune tellers shouting for customers in New Orleans, I was awake. Through the oil fields of Galveston, riding I am sure over an ocean of black gold, the air thick with its pungent smell, I was awake. In the Mexican restaurants of San Antonio, where bright-eyed, golden-skinned youngsters served us warm tortillas and spicy frijoles, I was awake. On the deserted two-lane highways of north Texas, through the rice-growing fields of Arkansas I was awake, and across the wide and slowly flowing Mississippi River and into Tennessee and Kentucky, across the muddy Ohio River and into Ohio, I was awake. It was glorious.

How I hope that this day, no matter where you are or what your condition is, you are awake!

Let me go a step further. No matter what your condition is, no matter what disease you have, no matter how close you are now to that ultimate last breath, there is still one thing to consider. And it will change your life.

You may not be able to change your circumstances, but in every case you can change your attitude about your circumstances!

The Fifth Century A.D. Indian poet and playwright Kalidasa put it this way in a Sanskrit proverb:

Look to this day,

For it is life,

The very life of life.

It its brief course lie all

The realities and verities of existence.

The bliss of growth,

The splendor of action,

The glory of power –

For yesterday is but a dream,

And tomorrow is only a vision,

But today, well lived,

Makes every yesterday a dream of happiness

And every tomorrow a vision of hope.

Look well, therefore, to this day.

Powerful stuff, that. And, it seems to me that the idea this 1600-year old proverb posits so nicely, is a very large part of my own continued clinging to life.

Another friend put this to me recently: How can you feel bad for something you did when you were fast asleep? You can insert any word necessary for you in there instead of bad: guilty, awful, remorseful, regretful, dissatisfied, unhappy. You see, many of us were fast asleep for a very long time. It is our illness that has awakened us. What a gift! I need not feel guilty about things that happened to me, or even for what others did *to* me when I was asleep. Because I am now awake, I can now let those go, as they are but lingering dreams. When I awake each day, my dreams disperse like the fluff from dandelions in late Spring in a gentle breeze.

The monk Thich Nhat Hanh, in the *Bhaddekaratta Sutta* describes one teaching of the Buddha as follows:

> Do not pursue the past.
> Do not lose yourself in the future.
> The past no longer is,
> And the future has yet to come.
> Looking deeply at life as it is
> In the very here and now,
> The [wise one] dwells
> In stability and freedom.
> We must be [thorough] today.
> To wait until tomorrow is too late.
> Death comes unexpectedly.
> How can we bargain with it?
> (Hanh, 1990)

We cannot bargain with death, or with God however you see him or her. We may only *be*, and we can only be *in this moment in time*. It is by being in this moment that I may continue to live fully, no matter what my physical condition actually is.

Due to my heart condition, I still cannot lift over about ten pounds, though I once lifted weights and practiced Tae Kwon Do. I

93

can now do neither. I can no longer walk more than a perhaps 100 feet without rest. These are limitations, but they do not dominate my life. I have learned to make each step a comforting one, conscious of the lifting of my leg, the swing of it forward, the placing of my heel and the roll to my toes. I have learned to ask for help to pick things up from the floor I can no longer reach, and to ask young people to do for me what I cannot do for myself. I still ride my motorcycle! I still see a few clients each week in my practice, most of whom are younger than my grandchildren. I am diligent in my days, and not waiting for a fantasy of tomorrow, but living as fully as I can in each day remaining to me.

I no longer barter with God, or with death. That is a game in which I own no bargaining chips. I think, again, that my impending death, and my continuing grapple with my illness, have become gifts.

Let me conclude with this. I had a beautiful youngster in my office not so long ago who was about 11-years old. A handsome and intelligent child, he is wise beyond his years. He is a husky boy, with dark hair shading his deep-set blue eyes, his clear face almost constantly lit by a smile. With his mother's permission, I can tell you his name is Logan.

At the end of our last session together, talking with him and his mother, I watched him thoughtfully. Finally I said, "Logan, I hope I live long enough to see how you turn out." It was a simple wish.

He looked at me, and kind of tilted his head to one side. Then he said, "Maybe God will give you something *miraculous*." The emphasis was his.

My immediate thought was as genuine as his. I said that God already had; the miracle was him.

But the miraculous in my own life is not just that boy, who hugged me when he left my office, and planted a dry man-kiss on my cheek. The other hundred or more youngsters who have invited me into their lives in the last few years have been miraculous. Walking through dreams and nightmares, attention deficit problems, depression and anxiety, family problems and divorces, addictions and illnesses with all of them have been miraculous. I cannot imagine what the rush of those butterfly wings may bring.

But equally so is the fact that I am still above ground, that my feet reach the floor each day, that my long-suffering wife and I still enjoy each other, that my friends and I still motor loudly down miles and miles of highway together. It is a wonder that Spring has come again this year, that the forsythia are already in bloom, that the deep purple of hyacinths again protrude from darkened earth, that the robins have returned, that a cardinal has found a home in the maple tree in our back yard, that the black squirrels have proliferated again this year, eating all of the bird seed I put in the feeders. Life is miraculous! The richness and wonder of it all is miraculous.

My yesterdays have become dreams of happiness and my tomorrows, however few of them there may be, have become visions of hope. I pray the same is true for you.

And this year, I think I'll ride the motorcycle across Canada.

Neil Cabe

Spring, 2011

References

Alcoholics Anonymous. New York City: (1976). New York: Alcoholics Anonymous World Services, Inc.

Bluebond-Langner, Myra. (1978). *The Private Worlds of Dying Children.* Princeton, NJ: Princeton University Press.

Frankl, Viktor E. (1984). *Man's Search for Meaning.* Boston: Washington Square Press.

Mitchell, Stephen. (1991). *The Gospel According to Jesus: A New Translation and Guide to His Essential Teachings for Believers and Unbelievers.* New York: HarperCollins.

Mosers, Jeffrey. (1989). *Oneness: Great Principles Shared by All Religions.* New York: Random House.

Sinch, K.D. (1998). *The Grace in Dying.* New York: HarperCollins.

Smith, Rodney. (1998). *Lessons from the Dying.* Somerville, MA: Wisdom Publications.

Turow, Scott. (1996). *Laws of Our Fathers.* New York: Warner Books, Inc.

Wilde, Oscar. (1909). *De Profundis.* New York: The Knickerbocker Press.

Made in the USA
Coppell, TX
21 May 2020

26187365R00059